YOU
ARE THE
GENERAL II
1800-1899

GREAT DECISIONS

YOU
ARE THE
GENERAL II
1800-1899

Nathan Aaseng

The Oliver Press, Inc.
Minneapolis

The Oliver Press, Inc.
Charlotte Square
5707 West 36th Street
Minneapolis, MN 55416-2510

Library of Congress Cataloging-in-Publication Data

Aaseng, Nathan.
You are the general II : 1800-1899 / Nathan Aaseng.
p.   cm.—(Great decisions)
Includes bibliographical references and index.
Summary: Examines eight military conflicts of the 1800s and the
military decisions that determined their outcomes.
ISBN: 1-881508-25-0
1. Military policy—Decisions making—Juvenile literature.
2. Military history. Modern—19th century—Juvenile literature.
[1. Military policy. 2. Military history, Modern—19th century.]
1. Title. II. Series.
UA11.A272 1995
355.4'8—dc20   94-46910
                                                                     CIP
                                                                      AC

ISBN: 1-881508-25-0
Great Decisions V
Printed in the United States of America

99 98 97 96 95   8 7 6 5 4 3 2 1

CONTENTS

French emperor Napoleon Bonaparte (1769-1821), one of the greatest military minds of the nineteenth century, knew that the outcome of one battle could alter the future of a nation.

INTRODUCTION

This is the moment you have trained for all of your life but had hoped would never arrive. War has broken out. Your country is engaged in a life-or-death struggle, and you are in command of your nation's military forces. In the midst of this nineteenth-century conflict, you run into a dangerous situation that calls for decisive action. As you consider your options for handling this matter, you realize you are standing at a crossroads in history. The choices you make during the 1800s could decide the outcome of a bitter war or even affect the fate of your nation for centuries to come.

No one else can make the decision for you. You can listen closely to your advisers, and you can consult maps and intelligence reports. In the end, however, you are the one who must give the orders. And you dare not be wrong! As a military commander, you need to be something of a gambler. For war holds no certainties, and luck is something you cannot control. An unexpected event can cause the best-laid plans of military geniuses to blow up in their faces. For whatever reason, if one of your choices turns out badly, the blame will fall on your shoulders because the decision was yours to make.

This book presents a wide spectrum of military quandaries that occurred during the nineteenth century. Some chapters will ask you to plot master strategies for waging a war. Others will ask where to position your troops on a battlefield. You must watch for opportunities to *flank* an enemy—that is, to maneuver your army so you can strike your opponents from two directions at once. You must also keep an eye on your supply lines, which are stationed between battle sites and safe territory to bring additional supplies to your army. You must determine when to take extra precautions, when to take risks, and where to attack.

Throughout the eight chapters of this book, you will command various military forces in North America, Europe, and Africa. You will put yourself in the place of those you may admire and those you may despise. By getting inside the minds of these nineteenth-century military leaders, you will see how the history of the world has taken shape. You might even discover that, had you been a commander in the past, the world would be a very different place today.

1

THE BRITISH ARMY
AT NEW ORLEANS
January 1815

For the past two years, your country, Great Britain, has waged a half-hearted war against the United States while already locked in a furious struggle with France. Now, the British have finally defeated Napoleon Bonaparte's powerful French army—no thanks to the Americans, who had been trading supplies with the French while claiming to be neutral.

Even worse, your government suspects that many able-bodied British subjects had deserted their naval units during the war with France and escaped to the United States. To handle this tense situation, your country has seized several American ships to search for British deserters. In 1812, U.S. president James Madison retaliated by declaring war against your country.

The British government has now sent you across the Atlantic Ocean to lead a strong force that will teach the upstart Americans a lesson. The primary objective of this expedition is to capture the port city of New Orleans, which provides vital shipping access to the Mississippi River. This location is so important to commerce that former U.S. president Thomas Jefferson had declared (before the United States bought New Orleans and the surrounding Louisiana Territory from France in 1803) that the nation controlling New Orleans "is the natural enemy of the United States."

New Orleans is not an easy place to approach from the Gulf of Mexico, where your ships have anchored. A maze of swamps and bays circles the city, making passage difficult. You began your campaign in mid-December 1814 by defeating a small fleet of U.S. warships—called *gunboats*—that were stationed in Lake Borgne, which extends into the gulf east of New Orleans. Then, you landed soldiers on the west shore of Lake Borgne and discovered an unguarded marsh leading to New Orleans. Your force waded through five miles of swampland and came within eight miles of New Orleans before the Americans noticed that you and your troops were there.

A hastily organized U.S. force then rushed to stop your advance. Without warning, the Americans charged out of the woods and attacked your men in the dark of night only a few days earlier. After a fierce fight, the U.S. soldiers retreated. Now, in the first week of January 1815, they have taken up defensive positions in front of you along the Rodriguez Canal. In order to get to New Orleans from your present position, you must break through their line of defense.

Serving as a link between the Mississippi River and the Gulf of Mexico, the city of New Orleans became critical to the economic growth of the United States. A victory at New Orleans could be a turning point in the War of 1812.

THE OPPOSING FORCES

Surrounded by the Mississippi River on one side and swampy bayous on another, a small group of U.S. soldiers now holds a strong defensive position. This allows them to concentrate their fire along a narrow strip of land. Led by Major-General Andrew Jackson, the forces are situated behind a dry ditch that is about two feet wide and from four to eight feet deep. The soldiers are hard at work with their shovels trying to strengthen the dirt walls that protect their base. A narrower stretch of passable land is located on the far bank of the Mississippi River. You are not certain how many men Jackson has in front of you or whether he has any troops stationed somewhere in the swampland behind you.

The United States controls passage of the river with two small warships. Cannon fire from these ships could shower destruction on the portion of the battlefield closest to the river. The Americans also have Fort St. Philip downstream as protection against your British warships coming upriver.

Your veteran army does not have much respect for the U.S. Army as a fighting force, especially compared to Napoleon Bonaparte's disciplined French army that your troops recently defeated in Europe. While your soldiers are known as the "redcoats," you call the U.S. defenders the "dirty shirts" because of their apparent lack of organization and discipline. Nevertheless, the Americans proved to be expert marksmen earlier in the war. Their military ranks include Choctaw Indians, who are skilled at fighting in thick woods, and professional pirates led by Jean Lafitte, who are experienced at firing cannon. The

In late 1814, notorious smuggler Jean "John" Lafitte (1780-1826?) turned down a request to aid the British and decided to work for the U.S. force instead.

U.S. soldiers inflicted heavy casualties on your men during the first two years of this war, which began on June 18, 1812.

YOUR FORCES

With the defeat of the French, the world now recognizes the British as the most powerful military force in existence. In August 1812, soon after the war began, another group of British troops easily captured and burned the U.S. capital of Washington, D.C.

In mid-December 1814, your warships easily defeated the U.S. resistance off Lake Borgne. You landed 1,600 soldiers and were within a day's march of New Orleans before Major-General Jackson discovered you. British reinforcements have been arriving steadily, so you

On August 14, 1812, British troops invaded Washington, D.C., setting fire to the U.S. Capitol building and the president's home—known as the White House after being restored and whitewashed.

now have 5,700 seasoned fighters on hand, perhaps the strongest British force ever sent to North America.

On the negative side, you are not in an ideal position. In order to conquer New Orleans, you needed to get a strong force into place before the U.S. soldiers could organize to stop you. Unfortunately, Jackson moved quickly and halted your advance before you had enough soldiers on hand to defeat him. The success of his attack has angered your troops.

Now you are at the end of a difficult supply line. Several miles of soupy muck lie between you and your ships, which are anchored on Lake Borgne. Your most powerful warships are unable to assist you because they are too large to navigate the Mississippi River. Your smaller warships could get into the river but would face a fierce fight trying to get past the U.S. fort. For the moment, the two small American warships are left unchallenged in the water.

YOU ARE IN COMMAND.

How are you going to accomplish your assignment to gain control of New Orleans?

Option 1 **Launch an immediate all-out attack.**
Although the situation is not ideal for an attack, this may be the best opportunity you'll get. The longer you wait, the worse the odds will be against you. You have a powerful, well-trained fighting force at your disposal. Alexander Dickson, your chief engineer, believes you have enough weapons on hand to carry out a successful attack. Admiral Alexander Cochrane, who is in charge of the naval operations on this expedition, also thinks you can overwhelm the U.S. soldiers. If you have reservations about making the assault, Cochrane has boasted that he can "take the city with my marines and sailors, and the army can bring up the baggage."

Though strong in the middle, Jackson's defensive positions have flaws. About half of his soldiers, those farthest from the river, are out of range of supporting gunfire from his ships. Because the end of Jackson's fighting line tails off into a woody swamp, it does not have the solid entrenchments that you see in the center of his fighting line. This is an important opportunity for you.

Furthermore, the U.S. soldiers have only barely defended the other side of the Mississippi River. If you can move some troops and a few cannons to that side, you might be able to get around Jackson's defenses.

Option 2 **Bring in big guns from the ships and then launch an attack.**

Despite Admiral Cochrane's boasting, Jackson's battle fortifications will be tough to crack. The center presents the most imposing barrier. Your men would have to cross 2,000 yards of open ground in front of well-protected marksmen in order to get at the opposing troops. Your attacking troops will need plenty of artillery if they hope to charge that section.

You have some very large cannons on board your ships back on Lake Borgne that your men could bring forward. The labor through the swamps would be exhausting, but your men are tough enough and clever enough to handle the job. These cannons could pound Jackson's defenses, smashing through his soldiers' *earthworks*—the small dirt walls used to shield military forces from attacks. It will then be easy to thin the ranks of the U.S. soldiers in New Orleans. That kind of preparation will give your attack a much better chance of success.

Option 3 **Hold your position and establish a second front somewhere else.**

Hauling huge cannons from the ships through the bayous will be extremely difficult. You are not familiar with this region, and you cannot predict how much time and effort you will need to accomplish the task. Every day you have to wait for the guns to arrive is a gift to the U.S. soldiers opposing you, who will have more time to build their dirt walls higher and thicker.

Even if more artillery arrives in good order, it will not guarantee your victory. Heavy cannons are not likely to be as effective here as in most places because Jackson's troops are tucked behind small walls that will absorb the impact of cannonballs. Moreover, while you are trying to beat Jackson's defenses, his soldiers will be firing at you.

Keep in mind, also, that good officers know how to cut their losses. If your attack should fail, your cannons will weigh you down. You will either have to slow down your retreat—and expose your men to enemy fire—or abandon the guns to the enemy.

Finally, by declining to attack now, you admit that you cannot beat the U.S. militia without support from the cannons. What if these cannons do not produce the desired effect? How will you then persuade your men to charge?

A far safer action would be to improve your position, which you can do in two ways. First, you could send your smaller warships up the Mississippi River. If these ships can get past the U.S.-held Fort St. Philip, they will turn the battle in your favor. Once you gain control of the river, your ships can pound Jackson's troops from the side with cannon fire. Under those conditions, Jackson would not be able to hold off a frontal attack from your infantry of foot soldiers.

Second, you could divide your soldiers and land some of them at another position, perhaps closer to New Orleans. By doing this, you would force Jackson to watch the rear and the right and left sides of his army, thus weakening the defenses directly in front of you.

Option 4 **Retreat and try a different route.**

You are not in a good position for a fight. Your initial plan of attacking New Orleans from the south had a chance of succeeding only if you surprised Jackson and advanced to the city before the U.S. soldiers could react. You did surprise Jackson, but your initial force was too small to complete the job. Jackson reacted quickly and halted your advance. In doing that, he has turned your advantage into a disadvantage. Now you are stuck in a swamp, and an entrenched enemy force blocks your path. Moreover, this foe is familiar with the land and climate here. Your ships are far away and of no help. Your supply line from these ships runs through a barely passable bayou. A small group of Americans could easily attack this supply line and cut your lines of communication with the British fleet in the Gulf of Mexico.

Establishing a second front here would be senseless. You could make an advance from the south, but the Louisiana bayous would confine such an advance to the narrow strips of land that the United States can easily defend. Better to start over and approach New Orleans from the north. By positioning your troops between New

Orleans and the rest of the United States, you would cut off the city from U.S. supplies and reinforcements. Your powerful fleet could then form a blockade against any assistance from the south.

A recent attempt to follow this plan had failed. But that was only a half-hearted attack on Fort Beyers by fewer than 100 men. Your army would have no difficulty. Jackson's army would try to stop you, but at least you would be fighting on more favorable ground than in the miserable Louisiana swamps.

On the negative side, however, a retreat of any kind would demoralize your troops. The thought of running away from a fight with the "dirty shirts" would humiliate them.

THE DECISION IS YOURS.
WHAT WILL YOU DO?

Option 1 Launch an immediate all-out attack.

Option 2 Bring in big guns from the ships and then launch an attack.

Option 3 Hold your position and establish a second front somewhere else.

Option 4 Retreat and try a different route.

Sir Edward Michael Pakenham (1778-1815), who had entered the British army in 1794, fought with distinction against Napoleon Bonaparte's French army before leading the British attack on New Orleans.

Sir Edward Pakenham chose *Option 2*.

When General Edward Pakenham took command following Jackson's surprise night attack in December 1814, he did not like what he found. Pakenham—who had suffered only two minor wounds since joining the British army in 1794—believed that, upon landing in North America, the British army should have aggressively proceeded toward New Orleans and established a second front of soldiers. But now that the British army was situated in an unfavorable position, Pakenham decided to make the best of matters. Admiral Cochrane's scornful dismissal of the possibility of retreat cramped Pakenham's desire to pursue any option except to attack. The question was whether to attack immediately or to wait for the guns or for support from the warships coming upriver.

On January 8, 1815, Pakenham ordered an immediate attack on Jackson's defenses. But he refused to commit himself to this course of action. He questioned the claim of chief engineer Dickson that the British artillery could support the assault. At the first sign of stiff resistance, Pakenham backed off. He believed that his cannons could soften up the U.S. defenses. Only after battering these defenses would he attack in force.

RESULT

Through a back-breaking effort, the British managed to haul in the light cannons from their ships. But by the time they reached the U.S. forces, more than 2,000 men from the Kentucky militia had arrived to assist Jackson's men. The Americans had also used the time to construct an eight-foot thick wall—called a *rampart*—to establish a defense on the far side of the river. U.S. sharpshooters turned the week into a reign of terror. They sneaked in under cover of dark and picked off British sentries.

The battle proved disastrous for the British. Although they knocked out one of the U.S. warships, they barely dented the U.S. land defenses. When the British cannonballs hit the American ramparts, they became stuck in the thick, wet mud. The U.S. soldiers, in fact, sent a more devastating fire at the British than they absorbed themselves.

Since he had planned to postpone the attack until the British forces had weakened their opponents, Pakenham had to decide what to do once his cannons had accomplished nothing. British major Harry Smith urged Pakenham to admit the situation was bleak and to withdraw the troops. But to ask his experienced soldiers to retreat in the face of the "dirty shirts" was something Pakenham could not do. "We are strong in numbers," Pakenham declared. "It will cost more men, but the assault must be made."

At that point, Pakenham's force numbered about 5,700 men. Jackson had nearly 5,000 men, although few of the Kentucky reinforcements were armed. Pakenham's plan called for 1,400 soldiers to cross the Mississippi River, take the artillery Jackson had positioned there, and turn them against the American forces.

Meanwhile, the rest of the British force, under generals John Keane and Samuel Gibbs, would charge directly at the U.S. fortifications and scale them with ladders.

The British had problems getting their soldiers across the river. Then, General Gibbs's men realized they had committed a horrendous blunder by forgetting to bring the scaling ladders with them. The British army had almost no chance of winning the battle and suffered staggering losses before abandoning the attempt and retreating back to their ships. In the Battle of New Orleans, the U.S. troops killed or wounded more than 2,500 British soldiers and took 500 more prisoners. General Pakenham and General Gibbs both died on the battlefield. Meanwhile, the British killed only 13 U.S. soldiers and wounded another 39.

Although the Battle of New Orleans is the most famous military conflict of the War of 1812, the war was officially over by the time the battle began. Diplomats for the two countries had already agreed to end the war by signing the Treaty of Ghent on December 24, 1814. But before the invention of the telegraph, messengers on horseback needed about two weeks to travel the 1,000 miles from Washington, D.C., to New Orleans. Word of the peace treaty did not reach New Orleans until a few days after the battle had ended.

The Battle of New Orleans helped establish the young United States, once and for all, as a strong, independent nation. Henry Garland, a captain in the U.S. Army at New Orleans, noted that most people considered July 4, 1776, as the day the founders of the United States officially declared independence from Britain. Garland, however, asserted that such a belief was

Sir Edward Pakenham died on January 8, 1815, while leading the British attack on New Orleans— two weeks after the War of 1812 had officially ended.

incorrect. To him and many others, the United States was not truly independent until the country secured New Orleans.

ANALYSIS

Some historians believe General Pakenham made a serious error in waiting to attack during the Battle of New Orleans. Hauling their cannons across land gained the British nothing but aching muscles and provided Jackson's force six days to turn his hastily prepared defenses into a fortress of mud, cotton, and straw. From this shelter, the U.S. troops could easily push back the British.

Jackson constantly worried that his defensive line on the Rodriguez Canal made him vulnerable to a second force coming in from another direction. But Pakenham would have had great difficulty establishing a second front from that position because the British forces were cramped into a spot where maneuvering was almost impossible.

Later events proved the futility of waiting for help from warships on the river. After the defeat at New Orleans, Admiral Cochrane sent a small naval force out against Fort St. Philip. That fleet repeatedly failed in its

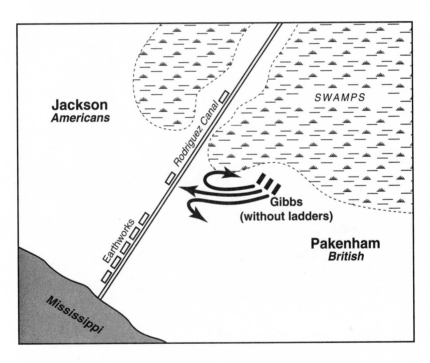

Advancing over open terrain toward well-fortified American positions proved devastating for the brave but badly led British army.

efforts to sail past the fort unharmed. Had Pakenham expected much help on that front, he would have been disappointed.

General Jackson was dumbfounded when the British attempted to capture New Orleans from the south. Jackson knew that if the British army had taken control of Mobile, about 140 miles to the northeast, the soldiers could have foraged off the land and cut off New Orleans from the north. Such an action, however, would have been difficult for a courageous British officer to accept. In the final attack, the British did overrun the U.S. defenses on the far side of the river. Had this been coordinated with a strong frontal attack against incomplete defenses and had Jackson's left flank collapsed, the U.S. soldiers would not have been able to hold their ground.

Andrew Jackson (1767-1845) became a national hero after his victory at the Battle of New Orleans. That attention helped him to become president of the United States in 1829.

2

THE PRUSSIAN ARMY AT WATERLOO
June 1815

Napoleon Bonaparte, who once dreamed of conquering Europe, escaped from exile on the Mediterranean island of Elba in February this year and returned to his native France in March. Determined to expand the French Empire, this military genius dominated Europe for more than a decade before the combined forces of several European powers finally defeated him last year. But the Napoleonic Wars have not ended. Bonaparte, who has regained control of the French army, is now plotting to defeat Britain and Prussia.

Although Bonaparte has rebuilt his shattered forces into a powerful army, this new army is by no means as intimidating as was his force during the first few years of the century. At the moment, Bonaparte is looking for a quick military victory to improve his bargaining position with his European neighbors.

Bonaparte has marched north from Paris to tackle two foes: your Prussian army and the British army, which

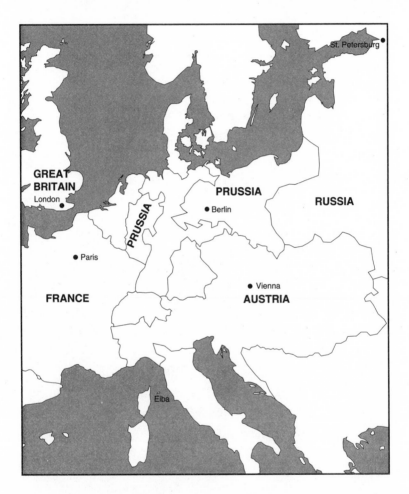

In 1815, the five great powers of Russia, Austria, Prussia, France, and Great Britain dominated Europe.

both have troops in what is now the country of Belgium. He moved so quickly and aggressively that he caught you and your British allies off guard. Now—the middle of June in 1815—part of his army has beaten your army at the Belgian town of Ligny and nearly destroyed it. Your Prussian soldiers are frantically trying to regroup. A smaller French force attacked the British army at the nearby village of Quatre Bras and forced the British to fall back. If torrential rains had not slowed their pursuit, the French troops might have overwhelmed the British.

France is well on its way to destroying both Prussia and Great Britain. Bonaparte has forced himself between your army and your ally, the British army. Now he is in position to finish off your troops and the British forces one at a time.

French marshal Michel Ney (1769-1815), who led France's successful attack on the British at Quatre Bras, was called "the bravest of the brave" by his commander, Napoleon Bonaparte.

THE OPPOSING FORCES

Napoleon Bonaparte's Army of the North has approximately 125,000 soldiers—many of them seasoned veterans of previous military campaigns. Surrounded by strong enemies, the French are now fighting with grim desperation. The key figure in this struggle is Bonaparte himself. As proven by his long string of decisive victories, he is a master of military strategy. British commanders concede that Bonaparte's mere presence on a battlefield is worth 40,000 soldiers.

One of Bonaparte's trademarks is his ability to keep his enemies off balance. He does this by spreading out his forces until the last possible moment so his enemies cannot predict where he will strike. Then, he marches his army swiftly to the attack point before his foes can react.

Although many observers suspect Bonaparte's abilities have slipped since his days of glory, his maneuvering in the past few days has been reminiscent of his past strategies. If Bonaparte has a weakness, it is arrogance. He thinks so highly of his ability that he sometimes believes his armies can accomplish more than they possibly can.

Presently, Bonaparte has placed a strong force in front of you, commanded by French marshal Emmanuel Grouchy. But a large part of Bonaparte's army is off to the west in the vicinity of the British force. Not only do the French outnumber the British, but they easily have the advantage in military leadership. Bonaparte is not one to let an opportunity pass. He is certain to proceed with the attack against the British while he has the stronger force.

Napoleon Bonaparte (on horseback), considered a skilled commander while still in his twenties, planned to lead France to supremacy in Europe.

YOUR FORCES

The Prussian army nearly matched the size of the French army before the Battle of Ligny two days ago. Today, June 18, you are down to about 100,000 soldiers, and your units are in disarray. The British force of about 80,000 has moved south of Brussels, near the town of Waterloo in central Belgium. This is not exactly the best of the British armed forces, and many of the soldiers lack battle experience.

On the other hand, the commander of the British forces, Arthur Wellington—the Duke of Wellington—is a seasoned military officer. Wellington gained considerable fame for his leadership in Spain a few years ago, when his

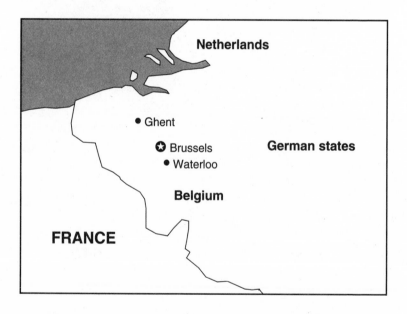

The French army began invading Belgium in June 1815, and battles are now taking place near the town of Waterloo.

Arthur Wellesley Wellington (1769-1852), who was knighted in 1805, led numerous military and diplomatic missions in both Europe and India before taking command of the British army in 1815.

forces consistently outmaneuvered and defeated their French opponents. Wellington is especially noted as an expert in tactics intended to defend against invading troops.

Bonaparte has made many enemies in his time. Large armies from Austria, Russia, and Italy are forming to the south and east of France. Although these forces number at least 400,000, they unfortunately are too far away to be of any assistance in the present conflict.

Wellington will need all of his expertise to fight off disaster. The duke doubts he can defeat Bonaparte in battle from his present position without some assistance from your Prussian army. But you are in a poor position to help. Your army is already fighting for its own survival against the determined French invaders.

YOU ARE IN COMMAND.

What move will you make to address the new threat of Napoleon?

Option 1 Retreat.

The sensible course of action is to get your Prussian army in order before trying to defeat any new opponents. Your army has taken a severe beating. Bonaparte could easily scatter your soldiers, thereby destroying your army as an effective fighting force. You cannot allow this to happen.

You would like to help Wellington. But with Bonaparte's forces in front of you, the only way you could reach Wellington would be to march past the French army, exposing your troops to fire from the side. No general relishes being put in that position. Wellington's desperate situation is his responsibility, and you would accomplish nothing by sacrificing your own forces to rescue his.

The joint forces opposing Bonaparte can survive the loss of Wellington's army. After all, the armies of three other nations are waiting to get involved in the action. However, the loss of both the Prussian and British armies would make other nations think twice about tangling with the French. If you and your forces retreated, you would not only save your own army but would benefit all of Europe. By retreating, you could live to fight another day.

Option 2 **Conduct a holding action.**

Sending help to Wellington would be foolhardy. Bonaparte could easily defeat Wellington before your reinforcements arrive, which would needlessly endanger your soldiers. Additionally, Bonaparte may be strong enough to win the battle with the British even if you go to Wellington's aid. In that case, you would have taken a great risk for nothing.

While you do not want to risk the fate of your army by sending some of your men on a futile rush to help Wellington's army, you may be able to help them by staying where you are. The French force under Grouchy, which is immediately in front of you, has only 33,000 men. Bonaparte might be concentrating so hard on Wellington that he will leave you alone for the moment. In that case, you could at least ensure that Grouchy's forces do not slip away and join the attack on Wellington. You should be able to regroup enough of your large force to engage Grouchy in battle and thus keep his army from closing in on the British troops.

Option 3 **Send a large force to Wellington's aid.**

Napoleon Bonaparte has said, "You must not expect luck if you are not bold." Now would be the time for a bold move that could destroy Bonaparte and end his menace once and for all. Despite the difficult position you are now in, you realize that together your Prussian army and the British army have the French outnumbered. Bonaparte has the advantage only because he has been able to keep his two foes separated so that he could batter them one at a time. Rather than concede him that advantage, you should do everything in your power to overcome it.

Bonaparte knows that he has essentially defeated your army. He probably expects you to retreat or at least to take time to regroup. He certainly would not expect you to march across the front of Grouchy's army and expose your soldiers to an attack. By doing the unexpected, you can surprise Bonaparte and turn the tables on him. If your army gets through and Wellington manages to hold out until you arrive, you will be able to crush the unsuspecting Bonaparte with the combined force of your army and the British force.

Option 4 **Send a small force to aid Wellington.**

The bold action of sending aid to Wellington is noble and daring, but you must avoid getting carried away. What if Bonaparte decides to turn on you and wipe out your army before he takes on Wellington? In that case, your march across Grouchy's front will hand him your army on a platter. Bonaparte could strike from the west, while Grouchy tears into you from the south and the east. You cannot hope to defend yourself in such a position.

On the other hand, what if Bonaparte defeats Wellington before your army arrives to help the British forces? Then your army will be caught between Bonaparte's force on the west and Grouchy's on the east. Again, your soldiers would be easy pickings.

Rather than become greedy by trying to spring a trap on Bonaparte, you would be wise to take a middle course of action. Wellington believes that he can fight off

Bonaparte with the addition of just a small force, perhaps a few thousand men. Take him at his word and send him only the forces he says he needs.

If Wellington is right, that smaller force will be sufficient to accomplish the job. If he is wrong, you at least will not have sent your whole army to destruction. The remainder of your forces would be able to pull out and eventually join the Austrians, the Italians, and the Russians, in stopping Bonaparte.

THE DECISION IS YOURS.
WHAT WILL YOU DO?

Option 1   Retreat.

Option 2   Conduct a holding action.

Option 3   Send a large force to Wellington's aid.

Option 4   Send a small force to aid Wellington.

Prussian marshal Gebhard von Blücher (1742-1819), whose troops had been defeated by the French army in Ligny on June 15, 1815, hoped to stop Napoleon Bonaparte's army at Waterloo.

Field Marshal Gebhard von Blücher chose *Option 3*.

Marshal Gebhard von Blücher—who had first joined the Prussian military in 1760 and had extensive combat experience—recognized that his army was not defeated as badly as he initially feared. When Bonaparte failed to press the attack against the retreating Prussians, von Blücher quickly recovered his nerve. He gambled that Bonaparte was concentrating completely on Wellington and that Grouchy's force would not act aggressively until Bonaparte was done with Wellington.

Von Blücher decided to do what he could to sabotage Bonaparte's strategy of splitting the Prussians and the British. He disregarded the advice of another Prussian commander, August von Gneisenau, who warned him that Wellington could not survive against Bonaparte at Waterloo. Leaving only 17,000 soldiers against Grouchy, von Blücher ordered more than 70,000 troops to march west to support Wellington.

RESULT

Napoleon Bonaparte believed that his victory at Ligny had eliminated the Prussians from the current battle. He left a moderate force of 32,000 men under Grouchy in the east to continue to drive back the Prussians and focused his energy on defeating Wellington.

On the morning of June 18, Bonaparte delayed his attack because wet ground hindered troop movements. This proved to be a costly delay. The first French assault did not begin until almost noon, by which time Prussian soldiers were beginning to march steadily toward Waterloo.

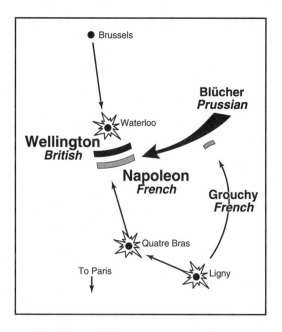

To help Wellington at Waterloo, the Prussians under von Blücher had to march in front of Grouchy's French troops protecting Napoleon's right flank.

Bonaparte launched wave after wave of attack on the British and their allies. The attacks were not well-coordinated, and the British fought skillfully under Wellington's inspiring direction and expertise. But the assaults eventually took their toll. By mid-afternoon, the British battle fortifications, which had thinned, were beginning to waver, and possibly ready to crumble.

By this time, however, Bonaparte was aware of the large Prussian force advancing from the east. Poor leadership by General Grouchy had allowed von Blücher's forces to slip past him. As the afternoon wore on, Bonaparte had to divert more and more of his soldiers to the east to protect against the upcoming Prussian attack. Several of his charges against the British threw back the enemy troops, but the French charges then sputtered out due to a lack of support.

As the situation grew desperate, Bonaparte put all of his best remaining troops into a furious charge at the center of the British line. The attack failed. By this time, the Prussian soldiers were swarming onto the battlefield and sweeping away the right wing of the French army. Wellington then sent his troops charging from their positions. The proud French army collapsed, and Bonaparte's soldiers fled back toward the south in complete disarray, more like a mob than an army. After fending off French assaults all day, the British were too exhausted to pursue the enemy. But the newly arrived Prussians pressed on, ensuring that Bonaparte's demoralized units could not reorganize. Three days later, Napoleon Bonaparte surrendered to the British, hoping to find asylum in their country.

The defeat at Waterloo spelled the end for Bonaparte. Instead of remaining in Britain, he was shipped as a prisoner of war to the island of St. Helena, located off the western coast of Africa. With the French military no longer a threat, the British became the dominant military power in Europe, a position they maintained for the rest of the nineteenth century.

The defeat of France at Waterloo—the last military conflict during the Napoleonic Wars—finally ended Napoleon Bonaparte's threat to other European nations.

ANALYSIS

Gebhard von Blücher took a serious risk in rushing to Wellington's defense during the Battle of Waterloo. That decision might have turned out poorly had Bonaparte been at the peak of his power. But the French leader overestimated the extent of his victory over the Prussians at Ligny. He refused to believe—until it was too late—that the Prussians would be able to offer the British any significant help. Many military analysts believe that Bonaparte would have emerged victorious if, before going after Wellington's British forces, he had first taken the time to finish off the Prussian army after the Battle of Ligny.

The haughty Bonaparte certainly never dreamed that von Blücher would be bold enough to attempt a march across the front of Grouchy's army. In the past, most of Bonaparte's enemies had been too fearful to attempt such a daring maneuver.

Furthermore, von Blücher had benefited from Bonaparte's vague orders to Marshal Grouchy. Unclear as to what Bonaparte wanted him to do, Grouchy failed to take a position that would have put him between Bonaparte and the Prussians. Had he done what Bonaparte had intended, Grouchy not only would have stopped von Blücher from aiding Wellington but would also have been able to send some troops to support the French attack at Waterloo.

Even with the Prussians' assistance, the British came perilously close to defeat at Waterloo. Wellington later admitted, "In all my life I have not experienced such anxiety, for I must confess I have never been so close to defeat." Had Bonaparte coordinated the attacks of both his infantry and cavalry more efficiently, he might have succeeded. Additionally, had he begun the attack earlier in the morning, he would not have had to draw off troops to defend against the advance of von Blücher and might have won the battle before the Prussian forces arrived.

In short, had the French avoided any one of a number of blunders, they might have won the Battle of Waterloo before the Prussians arrived. In that case, von Blücher would have sent his army, totally unsupported, into the powerful hands of the French army. History would have recorded his decision as a tragic blunder. Such was the risk that von Blücher had run. But with luck on his side, his boldness paid off.

Napoleon Bonaparte died of cancer on May 5, 1821, and his remains were shipped from St. Helena to Paris 19 years later. Despite his defeat at Waterloo, he is still regarded as one of history's most skillful military strategists.

3

THE UNITED STATES ARMY IN MEXICO
August 1847

Since last year, the United States and Mexico have been at war over the disputed territory that lies between the two countries alongside Texas. The United States does not have a strong military tradition. Except for minor conflicts with the native Indian tribes, the U.S. Army has not been involved in any military action since the Battle of New Orleans in 1815. The U.S. soldiers, however, have performed remarkably well during the war with Mexico.

The initial cause of the Mexican War was the annexation of Texas in 1845, when the Texas region became a U.S. state. Worried that the United States will try to acquire more territory, Mexican officials have refused the

United States' offer to use diplomacy to end the war peacefully. The United States has responded by launching an assault deeper into Mexico.

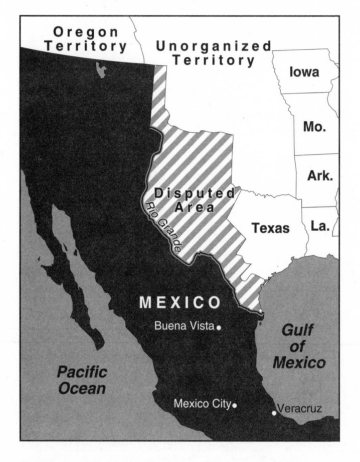

Beginning in 1846, the United States waged war against Mexico, in part because of a disagreement over the boundary of Texas. Major battles have already been fought at Veracruz and Buena Vista, and a confrontation in Mexico City now seems imminent.

Last year, during the early stages of the Mexican War, an army led by General Zachary Taylor defeated the Mexican army in a series of battles near the Texas border. This past March, you landed a strong American force by ship at the Mexican port city of Veracruz on the Gulf of Mexico. This army captured the powerful Mexican fortress at Veracruz with surprising ease. In April, your army set off westward in the direction of Mexico City, the capital. En route, you led your troops to a spectacular victory over a Mexican army at the Cerro Gordo mountain.

Your army's arrival in the port city of Veracruz in March 1847 met with weak Mexican resistance.

Despite your successes, you find yourself in a difficult situation. Now located in a foreign country, your army has moved uncomfortably far inland from Veracruz, which is your only source of supplies from home. Veracruz is a dangerous place to station your troops because of the widespread outbreaks there of yellow fever, a deadly disease that many soldiers call "black vomit" because of one of its symptoms.

THE OPPOSING FORCES

Even though the United States has a larger population than Mexico, the Mexicans are far from helpless. In fact, because you are fighting the war far from any U.S. city, the Mexican army has many more soldiers available for battle than you have. Even after suffering defeats near the Texas border, at Veracruz, and then at Cerro Gordo, the Mexicans have approximately 30,000 able soldiers who could attack you before you reach Mexico City.

The Mexican soldiers, however, suffer from ineffective leadership and poor morale, in part because of their dictator and military leader Antonio Santa Anna. According to disgruntled subordinates, General Santa Anna is a vain man who spent more money on outfitting his army in fancy uniforms than in providing them with new equipment. His disastrous planning at Cerro Gordo recently, along with his defeats at other battles during this war, must cause his soldiers to question his abilities.

The Mexicans are holding a strong defensive position to protect themselves from your army. A series of lakes and marshes protect Mexico City from the east.

During the Mexican War, General Antonio Santa Anna (1794-1876), who took command of Mexico in 1824, grew frustrated by his soldiers' early defeats.

These impassable areas will eliminate your ability to maneuver and will limit your options. On these shelter-less stretches of ground, your long, narrow lines of soldiers will make easy targets for concentrated enemy fire.

More than 300 miles of desert to the north separate the U.S. forces near the Texas border from Mexico City. Additionally, you know of no road that crosses a gray lava field, known as the *pedregal*, that lies to the south of Mexico City. This hardened area of lava has countless sharp ridges, which makes travel very difficult and will limit your ability to maneuver. The Mexicans will be able to attack in a few key spots, where they can inflict terrible casualties on your army.

Yellow fever, however, is potentially more dangerous than the Mexican army. The Veracruz area is a hotbed of this deadly disease, which is spread by infected mosquitoes. Fortunately, the disease does not appear to be as common in the highlands between Mexico City and Veracruz.

A final problem is the presence of Mexican bandits, who flourish in the sparsely inhabited, hilly countryside between Veracruz and Mexico City. Their ambushes can take a high toll on your supply line.

YOUR FORCES

Your numbers have fluctuated wildly in recent months. You frequently hear promises of U.S. reinforcements landing at Veracruz. One contingent of 2,500 soldiers did arrive there recently, but they did not even make up for the 4,000 volunteers who headed home in May when their term of enlistment was up. Currently, your fighting strength stands at about 10,000 men. This is a small force considering that you may need to seize Mexico City, which is populated by 200,000 people.

Thanks to two innovative elements, however, your army has performed remarkably well. Your engineers positioned their cannons and other artillery so effectively at Veracruz that your infantry never had to storm the walls of the city. The shell-shocked Mexicans surrendered the city without a fight.

The recent victory at Cerro Gordo was even more impressive. There, Santa Anna held the rugged mountain passes that blocked your path toward Mexico City. The Mexican general not only enjoyed a huge advantage in defensive strategy, but he also had more soldiers than your advancing U.S. Army. At the least, the U.S. Army would have suffered frightful losses without your engineers, who managed to haul cannons up hills that, according to Lieutenant Ulysses S. Grant, "were so steep that men could barely climb them. Animals could not."

Lieutenant Ulysses S. Grant (1822-1885) would continue to face new challenges long after the Mexican War—as commander of the Union army during the Civil War and as president of the United States from 1869 to 1877.

Never dreaming that an opposing army could survive in such impossible terrain, Santa Anna left part of his army temporarily unguarded. Overwhelming the defenders, the U.S. Army killed more than 1,000 Mexican soldiers and captured 3,000 prisoners and 40 guns. During the battle, only 400 U.S. soldiers lost their lives.

Your military superiority over the Mexicans has been consistent. Mexico's casualties in most encounters have been much higher than the losses of the United States. This is due, in part, to your "flying artillery"— sets of small, light cannons that soldiers can wheel in and out of position quickly. In this war, these small cannons have been far more effective than the Mexicans' heavier, less mobile artillery.

Your army is presently divided into two groups, which are 90 miles apart. This spread occurred because you are trying to maintain a supply line to your soldiers as they move inward from Veracruz toward Mexico City.

YOU ARE IN COMMAND.

What is your next move in this war of wills between two neighboring countries?

Option 1 **Fall back to defensive positions and hold the territory.**

General Zachary Taylor, who commanded the successful U.S. attack near the Texas border earlier this year, recommends taking this action. You have already accomplished a great deal in this war. You have decisively beaten

Mexico's armies and seized Mexican territory. The safest course of action is simply to hold on to that territory until the Mexicans work with your government to find a peaceful end to the conflict.

You must avoid pushing your luck. The Mexican army, though not a polished outfit, is still dangerous. This army pushed Taylor's troops perilously close to disaster at the Battle of Buena Vista in February, but the Mexicans withdrew after two days of fighting. You would be foolish to take chances against this foe, who outnumbers you. Any approach your small force makes toward Mexico City would run a large risk of failure.

Option 2 **Advance cautiously on Mexico City but guard your supply lines from Veracruz.**

Politically, holding on to Mexican territory indefinitely could cause problems. It would look as if you had grabbed Mexican land and were holding it for ransom. The military powers of Europe might consider that piracy and could consider aiding Mexico in its attempt to "liberate" its land. Furthermore, long stalemates often cause great unrest within a nation. The citizens of the United States were not unanimously in favor of this war to begin with. Many opponents of the war sarcastically refer to it as "Mr. Polk's War," since it was President James K. Polk who declared war on Mexico.

The longer the war drags on, the more heated the debate in the United States is likely to become. Also, a longer war means you will have more difficulty in obtaining the supplies your army needs to function effectively. As a matter of safety, you do not want to stay in Mexico a

James K. Polk (1795-1849), who would serve as president from 1845 to 1849, upset some U.S. citizens because, on more than one occasion, he risked putting the nation at war in order to acquire more territory.

moment longer than you have to. So far, you have been lucky in avoiding the dreaded yellow fever. But the longer your army sits in places such as Veracruz, the greater the chance that this disease will sweep through your ranks.

Finally, an army that does nothing but sit on captured territory suffers a drop in morale. The soldiers will grow bored and restless. The longer you remain on Mexican soil, the more trouble you are likely to experience between your troops and the Mexicans who resent having foreigners on their soil.

Probably the fastest way to bring this war to an end is to seize Mexico City, the nation's capital city. Your army may seem somewhat undersized to accomplish this task, but it has shown remarkable competence. The difficult terrain that naturally protects Mexico City can hardly be more challenging than the ravines of Cerro Gordo had been. You can count on your engineers to come through with some creative plan of attack.

The safest strategy would be to mount an offensive attack and seize Mexico City while maintaining a route back to your supply base at Veracruz. If the Mexican army should block that route, where will you get food and supplies for your soldiers? The best-trained army in the world cannot fight without food and equipment. As long as you are well-supplied, your army should be able to continue the success it has enjoyed. If your offensive attack against Mexico City fails, your army will at least be able to fall back along its supply lines and escape.

Option 3 **Abandon your base at Veracruz and move quickly to capture Mexico City.**

This is a huge risk for a small army struggling in a strange land far away from any possible support. If anything should go wrong—if the campaign should take longer than you planned, or if you suffer reverses on the battlefield—you would be unable to get back to your supply base at Veracruz in time. Then, you would probably have to surrender your entire army.

On the other hand, you would have great difficulty in trying to guard a supply line that runs through 180 miles of rugged, hostile Mexican territory. You would have to use hundreds of your men to guard against bandits. To have any chance for success in an attack on Mexico City, your outnumbered army needs to put every soldier at your command in battle. You simply do not have extra soldiers to spare for guard duty.

The job of capturing Mexico City is too difficult for you to attempt while also trying to keep in touch with Veracruz. So forget about the supply line. Take with you what you can. If you can continue to slash through the Mexican defenses as you have been doing, you may be able to capture Mexico City and end the war before your supplies run out.

Option 4 Order a smaller army from the north to join your attack on Mexico City.

General Taylor has established control over the disputed Texas territory of northern Mexico. You could summon U.S. soldiers in that region to advance on Mexico City from the north, while you march from the east.

This option would give you added firepower and would force the Mexicans to spread their defenses thin to cover all approaches to the city. A military rule of thumb is that the attacking force should be larger than that of the defenders to offset the defenders' advantage of prepared positions. Given the fact that you are significantly outnumbered by your enemies, the extra strength this option provides could be crucial.

On the negative side, General Taylor has declared that an invasion on Mexico City from the north is not practical. His army would have to cross 300 miles of desert, which would be especially dangerous during the August heat. Therefore, this option requires postponing your attack on Mexico City for several months.

You must keep in mind, however, that General Taylor has a track record of underestimating the U.S. Army. He was on record as saying that you would need 25,000 men to capture Veracruz, and you accomplished the task easily with fewer than half that.

THE DECISION IS YOURS.
WHAT WILL YOU DO?

Option 1   **Fall back to defensive positions and hold the territory.**

Option 2   **Advance cautiously on Mexico City but guard your supply lines from Veracruz.**

Option 3   **Abandon your base at Veracruz and move quickly to capture Mexico City.**

Option 4   **Order a smaller army from the north to join your attack on Mexico City.**

*Winfield Scott (1786-1866), who became commander
of the U.S. Army in 1841, had become a hero during
the War of 1812 and earned a solid reputation in the 1830s
for finding peaceful solutions to possible military conflicts.*

General Winfield Scott chose *Option 3*.

General Winfield Scott feared that the longer he stayed in Mexico without accomplishing something decisive, the worse his situation would become. Either U.S. officials would interfere with his plans, or Mexican bandits would attack, or yellow fever would finally take its toll. Scott did not believe that holding Mexican territory would bring about any concessions from Mexico. He agreed with Massachusetts senator Daniel Webster, an opponent of the Mexican War, who said "Mexico is an ugly enemy. She will not fight—and she will not retreat."

Scott thought it would be almost suicidal to have Taylor's forces march from the north through the desert in the middle of August. Faced with the increasing difficulty of maintaining his supply lines as he moved westward, General Scott decided to take a chance. "Finding myself isolated and abandoned, . . . always afraid that the next ship or messenger might recall or further cripple me," he wrote, "I resolved no longer to depend on Veracruz, or home, but to render my little army a self-sustaining machine."

RESULT

When Scott cut his supply and communications line and disappeared into the Mexican interior, most experts assumed he had made a tragic error. President Polk described Scott's decision as "a great military error."

Arthur Wellington—Britain's legendary Duke of Wellington—agreed. "Scott is lost," said the general who helped defeat Napoleon at Waterloo. "He can't take the city, and he can't fall back upon his bases. He won't leave Mexico without the permission of the Mexicans."

Scott succeeded, however, thanks again to his ingenious soldiers. Robert E. Lee discovered a way through the supposedly impassable pedregal from the south. Moving skillfully, the U.S. Army attacked the Mexican forces south of Mexico City. In a series of bitterly contested battles, the U.S. Army eventually forced its way to the outskirts of Mexico City, scattering the remaining opposition, and capturing the city in mid-September. The Mexican government then had no choice but to surrender on terms extremely favorable to the United States. Approximately 4,000 Mexican soldiers were wounded or killed during the attack on Mexico City. Of the U.S. soldiers there, only 133 were killed, 865 were wounded, and 40 were reported missing.

ANALYSIS

Scott had correctly read the mood of the United States. Even before Scott's march, former vice-president John C. Calhoun admitted, "The administration and the country are already tired of the Mexican War and are in as great haste to get out of it as they were to get into it." Because of that prevailing sentiment, Scott declined the option of holding on to Mexican territory. He also agreed with Taylor that a march from the north through the desert would be foolhardy.

As for the decision to cut his supply lines, Scott took a grave risk that nearly destroyed him. At the Battle of

Churubusco, near Mexico City, Scott waged a heated battle with a Mexican army more than double his numbers. Although the U.S. Army won the battle, more than 1,000 men died—about one-tenth of its fighting strength. After losing another 800 soldiers in September 1847 at the Molino del Rey outpost just outside Mexico City, the U.S. Army was perilously low in numbers. With another

General Winfield Scott, in the face of both political and military obstacles, risked his own reputation and that of the U.S. Army by advancing toward Mexico City.

such costly victory, the army could not possibly have succeeded.

When Scott reached Mexico City, he had enough rations for only four days. Had the troops been delayed anywhere along the line or had the engineers not found an unmapped route across the pedregal, Scott's great gamble could have backfired. But his tactics paid off.

Scott's daring decision brought an end to the Mexican War. In the 1848 Treaty of Guadalupe Hidalgo that ended the war, the United States added 500,000 square miles of Mexican territory to its borders, including what is now California, Nevada, and Utah, as well as much of Arizona and New Mexico. This represents one of the largest land acquisitions in the history of the world.

The Mexican War would continue until February 1848, almost two years after the conflict began.

4

THE ALLIED ARMY IN CRIMEA
September 1854

During the first half of the 1850s, the Turkish Empire has been slowly disintegrating. Various European nations have tried to gain military and political control of land in the Middle East and eastern Europe that was once controlled by Turkey. In July of 1853, when Russia seized Turkish-controlled territory in a dispute with the Turkish sultan over religious issues in the Holy Land, Turkey declared war against Russia.

Concerned about Russia's expansion into southern Europe, the nations of France and Great Britain joined Turkey by declaring war on Russia in March 1854. The conflict is now called the Crimean War. Working together, Turkey, France, and Great Britain have selected the port of Sebastopol (also called Sevastopol) on the Crimean peninsula as the target of their operations. Sebastopol is Russia's main naval base on the Black Sea. The Allies want to capture it and put an end to possible Russian outposts to the south.

Earlier in the war, a large British force and an even larger French force landed north of Sebastopol and advanced on the port. A strong Russian army under Prince Alexander Menschikov tried to stop the Allied forces at the Alma River, but the Allies soundly defeated the Russians, who are now fleeing back to Sebastopol.

As the leader of the French army, you must work with other Allied commanders to decide your strategy for attacking the Russian naval base at Sebastopol.

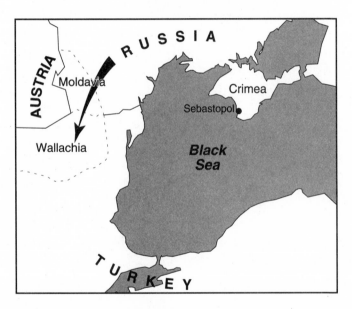

Russia's 1853 march into the provinces of Moldavia and Wallachia precipitated hostilities, which would largely take place in the Crimea.

THE OPPOSING FORCES

The Crimean War came about rather suddenly, and your military has had little time to prepare for an offensive attack on the Crimean peninsula. Therefore, you have almost no concrete knowledge of Russia's numbers or the strength of its defenses.

You do know that approximately 40,000 Russians took the field against you at the Alma River. Because they would not be likely to withhold a great number of troops from a major battle, you must assume that this was close to their total strength. The few thousand casualties that the Russians suffered in their defeat has now reduced this number to approximately 33,000.

The remaining units of Russian troops are retreating. Many of them are probably scattered, and Russia will need strong leadership to whip the troops back into fighting shape. The health of the Russian army, however, is basically intact. For some unknown reason, most of these soldiers stood idly by during the combat at the Alma River.

The scanty reports you have received indicate that Sebastopol may be well fortified with cannons and trenches. Though part of the Russian Empire, Sebastopol is a long way from Russian supply sources. A few Russian ships in the Sebastopol harbor—the side that appears to be best suited for defense—could help defend the city.

YOUR FORCES

Your French army consists of 40,000 troops. You are supported by a British force of less than 30,000, which is commanded by Lord Fitzroy Raglan, and several thousand Turks. The British soldiers distinguished themselves with a steady, courageous performance at the Alma River. Many of the officers, however, are either well past their prime or are inexperienced. Your French army was not as heavily involved in the fighting at the Alma River, and your soldiers are hoping to see some action.

You know that in numerous wars more soldiers have died from diseases than from battle wounds. At present, cholera poses a serious threat to your troops. People catch this infectious disease by consuming food or water that has been contaminated by bacteria. Because people suffering from cholera often die within a few weeks, you wonder how much longer your troops will remain healthy enough to fight.

Any invading army far from home must concern itself with maintaining a proper supply line. Your supplies must come by sea. This should not present any great difficulty because the Allies have both the stronger navy and access to the Black Sea from the Mediterranean. However, your army will have to keep a sea route open. Currently, that access is north of Sebastopol.

YOU ARE IN COMMAND.

How will you proceed in your attempt to capture Sebastopol?

Option 1 Press the advantage immediately.

The most decisive military victories occur when one army breaks through the other's lines and scatters them in confusion or panic. Your soldiers have just given you such an opportunity by overrunning the Russian positions above the Alma River. You have an almost entirely fresh army at your command to follow up on the British army's victory.

Such an opportunity is rare, and you would be foolish to waste it. You should rush your troops forward to pursue the retreating Russians. At the very least, your army should be able to scatter, capture, or destroy a large part of the remaining Russian resistance. At best, your troops may be able to advance all the way to Sebastopol and capture the city before the Russians have a chance to reorganize.

This option could prevent a long and costly campaign. If you allow the Russians to regroup behind strong defenses, you may have a terrible time trying to storm Sebastopol.

Option 2 Approach Sebastopol cautiously and attack from the north.

You have gained an important victory at the Alma River and now hold all the advantages over the Russians. Why risk all of that in a rash, blind pursuit of the enemy?

You do not know much about the strength of the Russian army, the state of its defenses, nor this area of land. If you rush headlong after the retreating Russians, you could easily fall into a trap. You know that the Russians have cavalry units that escaped the Battle of the Alma intact. A great number of Russian troops and guns may have been pulled back to better positions. The enemy could have a strong reserve force lying in ambush, ready to slaughter your overconfident troops.

History is full of powerful armies that lost crucial battles simply because their leaders got too carried away

When the Allied armies arrived in Crimea in September 1854—almost one year into the war— their primary objective was to capture Sebastopol.

by their success. You do not want to be responsible for destroying an army that is on the brink of victory. A far better solution is to march steadily but cautiously to Sebastopol and attack from the north. That logical approach allows you to stay in contact with your supply line on the coast. As you go farther south, the supply line will have to stretch. That is, you will probably have to land supplies at one of the nearby rivers. This is not ideal and could cause long-term supply problems. But at least you will have a clear line of retreat should you run into any unforeseen difficulties.

While Russian ships in the harbor at Sebastopol are in position to fire their cannons in support of the city's northern defenses, the British navy can deal with them. British naval commander Sir Edmund Lyons believes he can neutralize the Russians if you attack from the north.

Many people believe the defenses at Sebastopol are strong, but events of recent days indicate otherwise. Why would the Russians come out into the open and fight you at the Alma River? That action shows they must doubt the strength of their defenses. Therefore you should attack before they have a chance to build up those defenses.

Option 3 Advance cautiously and attack Sebastopol from the south.

Your scouting reports, although sketchy, indicate that Sebastopol's strongest defenses lie to the north of the city, along the east coast of Crimea. They appear to have a ring of trenches and artillery facing you from that direction. Obviously, the Russians expect that your attack will come from the north. Furthermore, your navy may not be able to provide as much help as the admirals think. The Russians have sunk warships at the entrance to the harbor to block your ships from entering.

If Sebastopol's strongest defenses face north, the wise course of action is to sweep across the peninsula and attack it from the south. Once again, you must do this quickly before the Russians discover what you are up to and have a chance to build their defenses. The last thing you want is to get involved in a long stalemate, with neither side winning—especially with the deadly cholera epidemic sweeping through the peninsula.

This involves a dangerous march in front of the enemy and forces you to re-establish your supply lines, probably on the southern coast. The roads from these ports to Sebastopol are terrible, and this could cause supply problems. But, for now, the shell-shocked Russians appear to be in no position to take offensive action against you.

Option 4 Surround Sebastopol and conduct a siege.

A head-on attack against a strong outpost is a costly, dangerous enterprise. This is especially true if you plan to sever your supply line on the north coast and set up an assault from the south. Since your Allied armies hold all the advantages at the moment, you can afford a safe play. That is, you can develop a plan that involves the least amount of risk to your soldiers. You see no sense in sacrificing many of your bravest soldiers in an open attack against concealed and protected defenders.

You can afford to take your time and use the standard method of attacking an outpost—the siege. Siege technique involves digging a series of trenches that bring you closer to the fortress without exposing your men to enemy fire. At the same time, you pour a steady barrage of artillery fire into the fortress to batter down the protection and weaken the resistance of those inside. When your trenches bring your troops close enough to the defenders of Sebastopol, you can launch your attack.

One drawback of a lengthy siege is that it requires a greater sustained supply line than does a short campaign. Thanks to the Allies' naval strength in the Black Sea, you should have no problem getting supplies to the southern coast. But the poor inland roads may become a greater problem as the siege wears on.

THE DECISION IS YOURS.
WHAT WILL YOU DO?

Option 1   **Press the advantage immediately.**

Option 2   **Approach Sebastopol cautiously and attack from the north.**

Option 3   **Advance cautiously and attack Sebastopol from the south.**

Option 4   **Surround Sebastopol and conduct a siege.**

French marshal Armand de Saint-Arnaud (1798-1854), who had joined the French Foreign Legion in 1837, served in India and in parts of Africa before taking command of the French army in the Crimean War.

Marshal Armand de Saint-Arnaud chose *Option 4*.

Unlike French marshal Armand de Saint-Arnaud—who had joined the French Foreign Legion in 1837 and had served under Louis Napoleon during the early 1850s—British commander Raglan favored *Option 1*. He urged de Saint-Arnaud to pursue the retreating Russians from the Alma River with his inexperienced troops. But de Saint-Arnaud, perhaps caught off guard by the sudden success of the Allied army, declined.

Proceeding cautiously due to a lack of reliable information, the Allied commanders decided that the northern forts posed too great a danger to their army. Judging that the ports of Balaclava and Kamiesch could provide supplies to the south that equaled their supply line on the north and that they could outmaneuver the retreating Russians with little difficulty, the Allies decided to move from the south. Comfortable with their superior numbers and position and fearful of the Russian defenses, the commanders chose the conservative route of a siege rather than risk an attack.

RESULT

The Allies encountered no resistance as they advanced from the Alma River toward Sebastopol. They completed their flanking movement successfully and established a French base at Kamiesch and a British base at Balaclava.

While the French and British prepared their siege, the Russians set about strengthening what were actually very weak defenses on both the northern and southern sides of Sebastopol. Your chief engineer, Franz Todleben, performed a masterful job preparing for the siege. Your men labored day and night to position your weapons and then to rebuild crumbling walls and construct earthworks for protection. Meanwhile, approximately 33,000 Russian soldiers arrived by ship to bolster the defense of Sebastopol.

While the French established a secure base at Kamiesch, the choice of Balaclava for the British base nearly ruined the Allied campaign. The British siege positions, located six miles from Balaclava, left them open to attack. On two occasions, the Russians attacked the exposed British lines in hopes of breaking the tightening stranglehold on their city. Fighting fiercely, the British, with help from their allies, managed to repulse both the attempts at Balaclava and also at Inkerman.

Heavy rains turned the only decent road to Balaclava into an impassable quagmire. While ships full of food, clothing, and medical supplies sat in Balaclava harbor, many British troops on the siege lines starved or froze to death. Then, a November storm destroyed British supply ships, causing a desperate shortage of food and supplies.

Equally dreadful were the cholera attacks. De Saint-Arnaud and Raglan both died of disease midway through the campaign, as did thousands of their soldiers. British reporters with the soldiers described grim scenes of squalor and deprivation, as well as the heroic efforts of a British nurse named Florence Nightingale to save as many soldiers as possible from cholera. Although the disease typically killed half of its victims, about 90 percent of those treated by nurses survived after contracting the disease.

Florence Nightingale (1820-1910), often considered the founder of modern nursing, organized a unit of 38 nurses to care for British soldiers during the Crimean War.

Six months into the siege, the Allies believed the time was ripe for an attack. They were wrong. The Russians repulsed the charge and the siege continued. Sebastopol held out for 12 miserable months. In the end, the Allies succeeded in their objective. After devastating the city with relentless bombardment and burrowing to within 30 yards of the Russian strongholds, they launched a full-scale assault. In bitter fighting in which the French played the major role, the Allies finally dislodged the Russians from many of their defenses, and the Russians finally evacuated the city.

The 1856 signing of the Treaty of Paris officially ended the war. This treaty re-established France as a military power and blocked Russian expansion to the south, thus ending Russian domination in eastern Europe. Nevertheless, only two decades later, Russia and Turkey were again at war over boundaries during the Russo-Turkish War of 1877-1878.

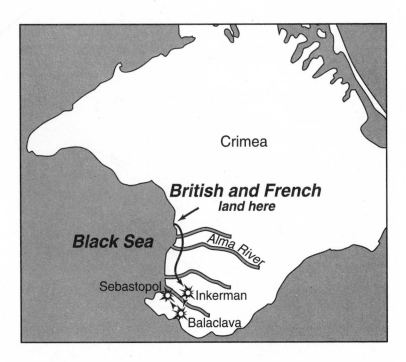

The Allied armies of France, Great Britain, and Turkey landed successfully in the Crimea about 30 miles north of Sebastopol, but cholera and a stubborn Russian defense would stymie their war goals.

ANALYSIS

Most historians agree that, in the long run, any of the other three options would have been better than the course the Allies chose during the Crimean War.

De Saint-Arnaud's subordinate commanders were livid at the marshal's failure to follow up on the Alma victory. Some historians contend that if the French had aggressively pursued the Russians at the Battle of the Alma, the campaign could well have been over in weeks. That conclusion echoes the opinion of Colonel Charles

After more than two years of fighting, the Crimean War came to an end in February 1856, when leaders from the opposing nations signed the Treaty of Paris, which re-established Russia's prewar borders.

Windham, a British participant at the Battle of the Alma. "The more I think of the battle, the more convinced I am that it might have ended the campaign," he later said.

Even though they let the disorganized and defeated Russians off the hook, the Allies could have redeemed matters with a quick assault on Sebastopol. Following the Battle of the Alma, Sebastopol was in poor shape to withstand an assault of any kind. The Allies' 70,000 troops should have been able to overwhelm the small Russian force there.

The best line of attack probably would have been the shortest one—from the north. The officer in charge of the Russian defenses later declared that he had only seven pieces of functioning artillery to fire at that time against an immediate attack from the north.

The chances of success from an immediate southern attack were also good. As Russia's Prince Gortschakoff said shortly after the battle, "There was nothing to stop the Allies from marching into the town."

The Allies' siege approach did eventually capture Sebastopol, and it avoided the type of monumental disaster that could have derailed the expedition. If the Russians could have fought off an attack, the expedition would have been in grave danger. But given the tremendous cost of the long siege, an immediate attack might have been worth the risk. The Allies' failure to seize Sebastopol quickly produced a miserable stalemate in which soldiers on both sides suffered terribly.

5

THE ARMY OF NORTHERN VIRGINIA AT CHANCELLORSVILLE
May 1863

For the past two years, the Confederate States of America have been fighting for their independence from the United States. You are in command of the Confederate army entrusted with defending the state of Virginia against the attacks of the huge, well-supplied Union forces of the federal government. Virginia's location between Washington, D.C., and the rest of the South makes the state the key battleground of the war.

This civil war—called the "War Between the States" in the South and the "War of Rebellion" in the North—began in the spring of 1861. Angered by the 1860 election of Republican president Abraham Lincoln, whose antislavery attitudes and other beliefs seemed like a threat to the rights of individual states, several southern states seceded from the nation. The U.S. federal government now claims that states do not have the authority to leave the nation. The first battle of this civil war between the North and South was fought in April 1861 at Fort Sumter in Charleston, South Carolina.

So far, your southern troops have enjoyed astounding success in your encounters with the enemy. Except for the Battle of Antietam last year, which basically ended

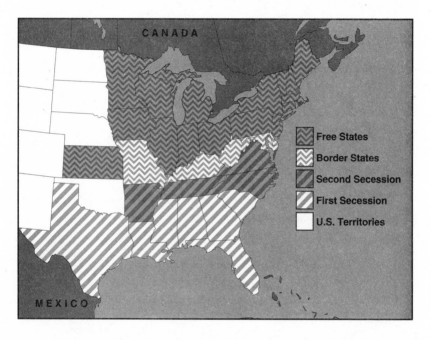

Seven southern states seceded from the nation between December 1860 and February 1861. Between April and June 1861, four more states joined the Confederacy. The border states did not secede from the Union, although slavery was legal in them.

Hostilities opening the Civil War began on April 12, 1861, when Confederate forces attacked Fort Sumter, a federal base in Charleston, South Carolina.

in a draw, your outnumbered Army of Northern Virginia has whipped its foes in every encounter. Last December, your army so badly mauled the attacking Union forces that observers on both sides described the scene as more like cold-blooded murder than warfare. The Union army, however, has now regrouped, and new recruits have swelled its numbers to more than twice yours. This powerful army is marching back into Virginia, looking to draw you into battle.

In previous battles, you have taken advantage of the terrain and positioned your army so that the Union armies had to cross rivers to attack you. Then, while they advanced over open fields, you fired on them from well-entrenched positions above the river.

Your forces are stationed just south of the Rappahannock River. But now your scouts report the disturbing news that you can no longer count on the river's protection. The Union soldiers have executed a flawless maneuver to the west and somehow have concealed this movement from your scouts. Now, a large portion of the enemy army is coming at you, unopposed, from the west.

At the same time, another powerful Union force is massed just to the northeast of where you are. Approximately 70,000 soldiers are now positioned in a forest area near Chancellorsville, Virginia. You are now

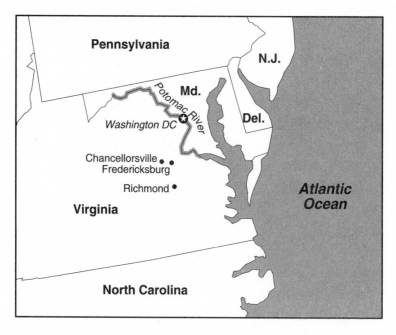

A decisive victory against the Union troops at Chancellorsville, Virginia, would help the Confederate army invade the North and perhaps win the Civil War.

caught between two parts of the Union army, each of which is at least as large as your entire army. Either one of these armies could attack at any moment. Your army holds the key to the survival of the Confederacy. If you suffer a serious defeat, your cause is lost.

THE OPPOSING FORCES

The Union troops have not fought poorly in previous battles, nor have they lacked courage. Their downfall has been the poor leadership of their generals. President Abraham Lincoln has been playing musical chairs with his generals, replacing one with another in hopes of finding one who can succeed.

So far, his efforts have been in vain. In fact, each new commander has been worse than the last. Major-General Ambrose Burnside, for instance, concocted a senseless battle plan at Fredericksburg in December that threw thousands of his troops into a slaughter pen in front of powerful Confederate positions.

President Lincoln has now replaced Burnside with Joseph Hooker. In previous battles, Hooker has lived up to his nickname of "Fighting Joe" by performing skillfully and with courage. Hooker has surprised everyone with his ability to rebuild the army and boost its morale after the disaster at Fredericksburg. Furthermore, his movement to the west without your knowledge was a superb piece of generalship. To his disadvantage, Hooker has never had overall command of an army in battle before. He also has the detrimental habit of boasting about what he is going to do before he does it.

Your scouts indicate that Hooker may have well over 80,000 soldiers under his command. At the moment, you are unable to determine which of his two divisions is the stronger. In addition to these forces, Hooker has sent George Stoneman's cavalry on a raid near the Confederate capital of Richmond, Virginia. This raid not only makes the Confederate government uneasy, but it could disrupt your supply lines coming out of Richmond.

Abraham Lincoln (1809-1865), who was elected president in 1860, faced opposition among his constituents in the North. Some northerners did not think the Union should be at war with the South, and others wanted Lincoln to make the abolition of slavery in the South a major objective of the war.

Union general Joseph "Fighting Joe" Hooker (1814-1879), a Mexican War veteran who also fought against the Seminole Indians, was honored for his bravery on three occasions. He left the military in 1853 but came out of retirement at the start of the Civil War.

YOUR FORCES

While you have to rely on educated guesses about the enemy's strength, you know the figures on your own army. The numbers are grim. After sending the 13,000 troops led by Lieutenant-General James Longstreet to the southeast to collect food and protect against reported Union movements, you have only 50,000 soldiers on hand for this battle. They have suffered through a dismal winter. They are badly fed and poorly clothed and are not as well-supplied with fighting equipment as their enemies.

Despite their hardships, morale among your troops is soaring. The men are proud of their battle success and fight fiercely, fully expecting to win every encounter with the enemy. They also trust and respect their leaders and follow instructions eagerly.

You have another advantage—the most exceptional field general in either army. In two short years, Thomas "Stonewall" Jackson has become a legend in both the North and the South for his daring, decisive action, and his unyielding will. Jackson is the perfect subordinate. He understands exactly what you want him to do, yet does not wait for orders when he sees an opportunity for success. His units have performed so many incredible marches that they have earned the nickname "foot cavalry." In several instances, they have showed up many miles from where they were expected, often just in time to turn the course of the battle.

General Thomas Jackson (1824-1863) became known as "Stonewall Jackson" early in the Civil War when he and his Confederate brigade stood "like a stone wall" against the Union soldiers.

The combination of excellent leadership and gritty, determined, skilled soldiers has made the Army of Northern Virginia one of the finest fighting forces the world has ever seen.

YOU ARE IN COMMAND.

What action can you take to get out of the dangerous position that you are in, stuck between two divisions of the Union army?

Option 1 **Retreat to stronger ground.**

Your army is outnumbered at least two to one. Under such a handicap, you desperately need every advantage you can get. In previous battles, you have always held a stronger defensive position, but the Union army has taken the advantage away from you.

In past encounters with this army, you have benefited from your opponent's poor leadership. While Hooker is still untested in his role as an overall commander of the Union army, his war record to date indicates that he knows how to lead soldiers. The brilliance of his maneuvers suggests that he is a confident man who knows what he is doing.

You are in a precarious spot between two strong forces. If you fight, you run the risk of being enveloped and crushed by your enemies. The Confederacy cannot afford to lose your army. In fact, your army is so important to the protection of the South that you cannot afford to lose any battle.

While a retreat may wound the pride of your army, a good leader knows that sometimes walking away from a fight serves a cause better than staying in position and fighting. This is one of those times. You should fall back to another river or a similarly strong defensive position.

Option 2 Divide your forces and attack where you are not expected.

The best weapon against a stronger force is the element of surprise. Hooker undoubtedly knows that he has the upper hand, and he expects you to retreat to safety. He would be surprised if you stayed around to fight, and he would be dumbfounded if you violated one of the fundamental rules taught in the military schools: Never divide your troops in the face of superior force.

This option carries an extreme risk, but then the whole Confederate cause is a long shot. If the war drags on for several years, the North—with its larger population and developed industries—will eventually wear down the South. Because of this, you cannot afford to play safe.

A daring, unexpected move may be the way to exploit Hooker's inexperience as commander of a large army and to end the war immediately. As long as you allow Hooker to proceed with his carefully orchestrated plan, he will become more confident in his new role. But if you go on the attack when he thinks he has you on the run, he may be so surprised that he will not immediately react to your move. If you are lucky, your movement could totally unnerve him. At the very least, you will force him to make quick decisions to counter your actions, and this will increase the chance he may blunder.

Option 3 **Consolidate your army into a strong defensive position and wait for Lieutenant-General Longstreet to bring reinforcements.**

Dividing your army merely reduces your force into bite-sized pieces for the enemy to devour one after another. This tactic increases the likelihood of a weak link somewhere in your fortification. Then, the Federal troops will break through and encircle your troops.

The only possible excuse for dividing your army would be to gather more troops than Hooker has. You can accomplish this only by taking large numbers of soldiers out of the battle lines and moving them to other positions, which would leave a skeleton crew behind. This strategy can be successful only if Hooker does not know you are moving troops. If he finds out, he can annihilate the thinned ranks left behind after you move your troops to other positions.

Unfortunately, concealing troop movement in this vicinity will be difficult. Most of the surrounding area is dense wilderness. If you want to move a division, you can do so only by sending it on roads so narrow that the soldiers will be spread out for several miles. The odds of moving such a long line undetected with the enemy so close at hand are slim. An equally grave concern is that if Hooker attacks during one of these troop movements, your soldiers will have trouble forming effective fighting ranks from such a spread-out marching formation.

In a wilderness region, troop movements are also hard to coordinate. A simple mistake in the timing of an attack could doom your army to disaster. Your soldiers have been unbeatable whenever they have taken up defensive positions. Therefore, the best thing to do is to stay in place to guard off enemy attacks.

Your army is still in command of the same positions near Fredericksburg and Chancellorsville that Burnside, the previous commander for the Union troops, failed so miserably to take this past winter. Let the Union generals and their troops try again. Meanwhile, attempt to set up a line of defense against the attack coming from the left. Your fine fighting units should be able to hold off the attack until Longstreet and his 13,000 men arrive to reduce the odds against you.

***Option 4* Consolidate your army and attack one of the two wings of the Union army.**

For all of the above reasons, you must avoid the mistake of dividing your army. Yet you do not want to be trapped in a defensive position between two strong attacking armies. A wise commander strives at all costs to avoid being surrounded and cut off from any possible escape route. As Stonewall Jackson says, "a defensive campaign can only be made successful by taking the aggressive at the proper time." You must hit Hooker with a bold offensive strike while keeping your forces together.

You can do this by attacking the Union forces to your right. General Jackson believes this division of Union troops led by General John Sedgwick offers an inviting target. If you work quickly, a successful attack against this set of enemy soldiers could drive off the enemy before Hooker's other division arrives from the west and put you in a much better position to deal with this western threat.

On the other hand, if you do not succeed soon, Hooker's western forces may arrive at your rear while you are in the middle of an attack. This would mean disaster for your army. The Union's powerful pieces of artillery up on the hills behind Sedgwick cast a strong doubt as to whether he can be beaten quickly.

THE DECISION IS YOURS.
WHAT WILL YOU DO?

Option 1   Retreat to stronger ground.

Option 2   Divide your forces and attack where you are not expected.

Option 3   Consolidate your army into a strong defensive position and wait for Lieutenant-General Longstreet to bring reinforcements.

Option 4   Consolidate your army and attack one of the two wings of the Union army.

After the first group of southern states seceded from the Union, Major-General Robert E. Lee (1807-1870) —a Virginia native— resigned from the U.S. Army in April 1861 to join the Confederate forces.

General Robert E. Lee chose *Option 2*.

General Robert E. Lee—a former superintendent at West Point military academy—believed in fighting aggressively and creatively. Instead of allowing enemies to carry out a plan of action, he liked to force them to respond to his moves. If this involved great risks, Lee was willing to take them. As one of his aides remarked, "Lee will take more desperate chances and take them quicker than any other general in the country." The presence of the brilliant military strategist Stonewall Jackson in the field increased the odds that Lee could get away with his gamble.

General Lee, who had fought with distinction during the Mexican War, refused to retreat even though Hooker's army was in a better position. Nor would he sit back and wait for Hooker to encircle him. Concerned about the strong Union forces to the east, Lee chose not to attack there. Instead, he gambled that Hooker's main attack would come from the west. Lee divided his army. Leaving a thin line of defense in front of Sedgwick, he marched the rest of his soldiers west to attack Hooker.

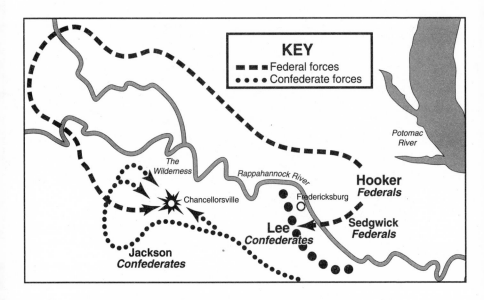

Leaving a small Confederate force behind at Fredericksburg, General Lee met the Union army's attempt to outflank him at Chancellorsville.

RESULT

Lee's attack, from May 2 to May 4, 1863, hurled 50,000 soldiers against 80,000 of Hooker's troops. Despite holding the advantage in both numbers and field position, Hooker surprisingly ordered his generals to halt their advance and fall back to defensive positions. Meanwhile, Sedgwick, unaware that the Union army was stronger than Lee's forces in the east, failed to take advantage of the mismatch.

Encouraged by Hooker's actions, Stonewall Jackson proposed dividing the Confederate western forces even further. Leaving a thin line of 14,000 troops in front of Hooker's vast army, Jackson proposed marching 26,000 men all the way around the western side of Hooker's army and attacking from the rear. Lee approved the risky maneuver.

Despite Jackson's efforts to keep the 12-mile march a secret, Union scouts detected the Confederates' movements. Hooker and many subordinate officers, however, assumed that Lee was retreating. They ignored the possibility that Jackson was marching around them. When Jackson suddenly burst upon the Federal soldiers from the west, the result was, according to an eyewitness, "an avalanche of panic-stricken, flying men," and "a wild frenzied mob tearing to the rear."

The Battle of Chancellorsville—which was fought from May 2 to May 4, 1863—was one of the Confederacy's greatest victories during the Civil War.

With the advantage of superior numbers, Hooker's army was eventually able to regroup and form solid defensive positions. At about this time, Sedgwick finally did overwhelm the Confederate position in the east. But Lee countered by dividing his army a third time, leaving a small force in front of Hooker and marching the rest of his men back east to drive off Sedgwick's troops.

The result was what Civil War expert Bruce Catton called "the most dazzling of all Confederate victories" over a force more than double the size of the Confederate army. More than 17,000 Union soldiers and 13,000 Confederates lost their lives. The outcome demoralized the Union troops. Had delays and some confusion in Jackson's march and side attack not occurred, Hooker's defeat would have been even more devastating.

Outside a Union army hospital in Fredericksburg, wounded soldiers await treatment.

ANALYSIS

Military experts agree that Lee could not stay where he was and allow Hooker's army to envelop him during the Battle of Chancellorsville. An all-out assault on Sedgwick's positions would have been doubtful at best. Even Stonewall Jackson, who originally proposed attacking on that front, changed his mind after studying the Union defenses more closely.

The only logical choice for Lee was to retreat to a better defensive position. In dividing his army, Lee went against the rules and took an enormous risk. Had Hooker behaved as one would have expected him to, given his previous record, Lee would have been in serious trouble. Had he gone on the offensive and attacked any time after Lee made his decision to divide his army, Hooker could have easily smashed through Lee's battle fortifications and probably destroyed his Confederate army.

Throughout the fight, most of Hooker's advisers pleaded with him to make such attacks. When Union general Henry Slocum received the order to retreat to defensive positions, he fumed, "Nobody but a crazy man would give such an order when we have victory in sight." If any of a number of Hooker's officers had been in charge instead of Hooker, Lee's decision could well have ended up as the Confederate leader's worst mistake.

Fortunately for the Confederacy, Lee had an uncanny ability to read his opponents. He had correctly predicted how Joseph Hooker would react to the unexpected action of the Confederate army. Hooker was

The seven stars on the Confederate flag symbolized the first seven states to secede from the Union.

convinced that his maneuvering had left Lee no choice but to retreat. "The operations of the last three days have determined that our enemy must either ingloriously fly, or come out from behind his defenses and give us battle on our own ground, where certain destruction awaits him," Hooker had boasted before the battle.

Lee's bold attack totally unhinged the blustery Union commander. After the battle, Hooker himself admitted that for once he had lost confidence in himself. Recognizing that Hooker was paralyzed by uncertainty, Lee kept taking more and more chances. Despite being greatly outnumbered, he repeatedly got most of his forces into the battles while many of Hooker's men never entered into the fight.

The Battle of Chancellorsville is one of the most striking examples of one general totally outclassing another. Many historians have called it the biggest success in Robert E. Lee's military career.

6

THE ARMY OF NORTHERN VIRGINIA AT GETTYSBURG
July 1863

Fresh off your victory this spring over Union general Joseph Hooker at Chancellorsville, your Army of Northern Virginia has struck off on a bold new venture during the Civil War between the North and the South. Your soldiers have invaded Union territory and have now entered the northern state of Pennsylvania. The Confederate leaders hope this drive into the North will confuse and disrupt the Union army.

If nothing else, the invasion will keep Union soldiers out of Virginia and give the people of that state a much-needed rest from war and destruction. With luck, a victory on a northern battlefield could frighten the people in the northern states, persuading them to seek peace as quickly as possible and allowing the South to establish its independence from the United States.

In warfare, however, great results usually come with great risks. By moving into the North, you have exposed your army to enormous danger. Part of the Union army could get behind you and cut off your line of retreat back to the South. If they then manage to defeat you in battle, you would have nowhere to retreat. You would probably have to surrender your army.

As advance units of the Confederate army moved into Pennsylvania, the troops ran into a small Union force at the town of Gettysburg, a significant location because of the many major roads that came together there. Reinforcements flowed in from both sides and turned the skirmish into a full-scale battle. As usual, the Army of Northern Virginia won the first engagement decisively on July 1, 1863. The troops pushed the Union forces back to a line of hills south of Gettysburg.

The second day of the battle, July 2, did not go well for your forces, however. At 4 P.M., your army made a furious effort to crush both ends of the Union's defensive line. At several points, the attacks came within a whisker of breaking the Union defensive walls. But in the end, these attacks fizzled out and produced nothing but a horrendous loss of life in both armies.

As darkness now falls along the battlefield, the Union army still holds a strong defensive position along the hills facing you from the east. The Union soldiers are solidly positioned at Culp's Hill to the north, Cemetery Ridge in the center, and the Round Top hills to the south.

After a series of successful battles in the South, the Confederate army has entered the northern state of Pennsylvania. The upcoming battle in Gettysburg could prove to be a turning point in the Civil War.

THE OPPOSING FORCES

The Union army camping on the opposite ridge is the same army that you have battered so decisively throughout the war. They are smarting from and demoralized by the humiliating defeat at Chancellorsville. Their numbers have dropped and are undoubtedly fewer than the number that marched against you two months ago.

Most of the Union soldiers, however, are probably more frustrated than intimidated by your mastery over them. They have been let down by incompetent commanders. Only days before the Gettysburg battle began, U.S. president Abraham Lincoln made his latest attempt to remedy that defect. Joseph Hooker had asked to be replaced from overall command of the Federal forces opposing you. Lincoln moved George Meade to that position. Meade has the reputation of being a tough and competent soldier, though neither as flashy nor as pompous as "Fighting Joe" Hooker.

For only the second time in the war, the Union army is defending its own soil. They are likely to fight more tenaciously and with greater confidence when protecting their home turf than when bogged down in a Virginia wilderness.

This Union army has assumed a strong defensive position south of Gettysburg. A common maxim in warfare is that the advantage lies with whichever side holds the high ground. The Union soldiers hold the high ground. So far you have not found a weak spot in their line.

George Meade (1815-1872) earned a reputation as a formidable Union general during the 1862 battles at Bull Run and Antietam.

YOUR FORCES

In some ways, your situation is more favorable than it was at your previous victories over the enemy. You have roughly 75,000 soldiers under your command. That puts your numbers at least reasonably close to the Union strength. This is the first time in many months that you have not been seriously outnumbered.

Although your attacks at Culp's Hill, on the north end of the Union line, failed to break through, your soldiers were able to advance on that front and are in better position to renew the assault than they were yesterday. A furious effort may put you over the top of the hill.

You also have the advantage of commanding one of the most effective fighting forces in the world. In spite of its inferior numbers and supplies, the Army of Northern Virginia has repeatedly defeated the opposing forces. The courage and skill of your troops is so strong that, at times, there seems to be nothing they will not try and cannot accomplish.

While many of your divisions have suffered heavy casualties and are battle-weary from the first two days of fighting, a division of 15,000 men led by General George Pickett has recently arrived and is eager to join in the fray.

The most serious concerns you have involve two of the most skilled officers in your army. General Thomas "Stonewall" Jackson was accidentally shot and killed by his own men during the Battle of Chancellorsville in May. The death of that resourceful and inspiring figure leaves a gaping void in the leadership of your army. That was apparent at Culp's Hill, where Jackson's replacement,

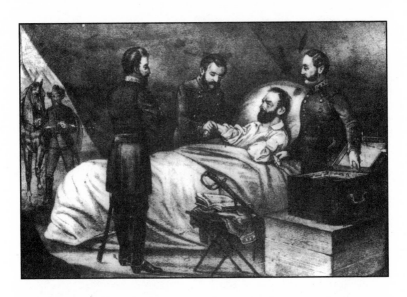

General Stonewall Jackson, whose military expertise had contributed to several Confederate victories early in the Civil War, died on May 10, 1863, eight days after being wounded by his own soldiers.

Richard Ewell, acted hesitantly on the first day of the battle and failed to capture that key objective.

In addition, Major-General J.E.B. Stuart's absence compounds your difficulties. Throughout the war, Stuart's cavalry has constantly probed the enemy lines, providing you with valuable scouting reports. Thanks to Stuart, you have usually known where the enemy was and how many enemy soldiers were at hand. By keeping between you and the enemy, Stuart and his cavalry unit have often screened your movements from Union scouts.

But this time Stuart is off on a scouting mission and unaware of the situation you face. To get himself clear of the enemy, he had to ride for several days in a wide circle far from your army. As a result, he has provided you with no scouting information on the Federal army. Stuart's reports are especially crucial when you are venturing into unfamiliar territory. You have no idea about the size of Meade's army in front of you at Gettysburg or what forces he may have in reserve to the east.

YOU ARE IN COMMAND.

What are your plans for the third day of the Battle of Gettysburg?

Option 1 **Sit tight and let Meade and the Union army attack.**

While you do not like to let the other side take the initiative, this time you have no choice. The Union positions look ominously similar to your defensive positions at the Battle of Fredericksburg last winter, when the Union lost 12,000 men—twice the number of Confederates that were killed.

That attack has proven beyond a doubt that improvements in the accuracy and efficiency of muskets, rifles, and cannons have made frontal assaults against strongly fortified hills pure suicide. A Union cannon loaded with *grapeshot* (a cluster of small iron balls that blows apart when fired) can instantly wipe out dozens of attackers. One of your trusted advisers, Lieutenant-General James Longstreet, flatly predicts that you cannot successfully assault the current Union positions.

You have no certainty that the enemy will move out of its positions and attack. But if Meade fails to let his army do so, he runs the risk of poor morale. His soldiers are plainly irate over poor, timid leadership. Your army so outfoxed Hooker at Chancellorsville that many Union soldiers never got into battle. After suffering that humiliation without even a chance to fire their weapons, many Union soldiers must be eager to prove themselves. They will not take kindly to any orders that ask them to sit and wait. Once you get Meade's army out in the open, you have a better chance of defeating it.

Option 2 **Retreat and find a different battlefield.**

While you may face heavy losses if you try to assault the Union positions, you are playing a fool's game if you think the enemy will go on the attack. Perhaps one of the former Union generals would have made that mistake, but Meade is a capable veteran who understands the situation. He also seems to be more stable than Hooker.

The fact is that you cannot afford to sit still and wait. You are in enemy territory, far from home and supply lines. Your army is surviving by living off the land. While the Pennsylvania farmland around Gettysburg is rich, it cannot feed 75,000 soldiers for more than a few days. The only way you can feed your army on this invasion is to keep moving. The Union army, on the other hand, can afford to wait because, in the North, the Union soldiers have easy access to food and supplies.

You need not risk your army on another costly assault on the Union line. If you can conduct an orderly withdrawal and get Stuart back to provide scouting reports, you will certainly find more favorable ground on which to gain a smashing victory—a victory that could force the North to ask for peace and end the war.

Cavalry commander James "Jeb" Stuart (1833-1864), who fought in the battles of Antietam and Fredericksburg, provided General Lee with valuable information about the size and position of enemy armies.

Option 3 **Try to outflank the southern end of the Union line.**

The proud Army of Northern Virginia has earned its success by being bold and aggressive. Retreating is hardly a bold and aggressive action.

Actually, the enemy has done you a favor by accepting battle. At least now you do not have to march around hostile, unfamiliar territory in search of an opposing force to defeat. If you decline this chance to fight, you may have trouble drawing the cautious Meade into a major battle. You cannot afford to stay in the North very long. If you end up having to turn back to the South without a significant victory, this whole venture will be a waste.

General Longstreet proposes a flanking movement around the Round Top hills at the southern end of the

Union line of defense. This is similar to the plan that had worked so well at Chancellorsville. You could throw your troops into the strength of the enemy defenses facing you. But why not divide the army and march part of it around the south to come at Meade from the rear? This flanking tactic offers less risk of the Union soldiers attacking the small force that you leave behind than there was at Chancellorsville because the Union soldiers in front of you have taken up obvious defensive positions.

Option 4 Launch a full-scale assault on the Union center.

The flanking option poses two problems. First, Stonewall Jackson is not here to lead the assault as he did at Chancellorsville. His peerless leadership made such maneuvers look easier than they really were. A coordinated assault from two separated wings of the army is actually very difficult to accomplish.

Second, when you maneuvered at Chancellorsville, you had a good idea of where the Union troops were. This time, you are groping in the dark. Jeb Stuart's long absence has left you without reliable reports of the enemy's strength and movements. If Meade has reserves in position to the southeast, your flanking movement could run into an ambush. Should that happen, the right wing of your army could be cut off and captured or destroyed by the Federal troops. You would then be hard pressed to escape from Pennsylvania with much of your army remaining.

You have won your battles by taking decisive action. While a frontal assault is dangerous and will likely cost you dearly in casualties, it may be just the bold stroke that carries the day. Your army is a magnificent fighting machine that can accomplish anything once your soldiers put their minds to it. They have routed this Union army many times before under difficult odds. Union officers have always been skittish around you—almost in awe of your ability. A bold frontal attack may surprise and unnerve them. They may break and run.

Furthermore, you can support this attack with several other tactics. You can direct your artillery fire on the Union line just before the assault. You can send General Dick Ewell's men back on the offensive at Culp's Hill and order Stuart, who arrived on the second day of the battle, to make a quick strike to the rear of the Union line. These actions will draw off troops from the center of the Union line where your main thrust will occur.

THE DECISION IS YOURS.
WHAT WILL YOU DO?

Option 1   **Sit tight and let Meade and the Union army attack.**

Option 2   **Retreat and find a different battlefield.**

Option 3   **Try to outflank the southern end of the Union line.**

Option 4   **Launch a full-scale assault on the Union center.**

General Robert E. Lee chose *Option 4*.

As the leader of an invasion force that was living off the land, General Robert E. Lee knew he had to keep moving. He could not afford to wait for the Union army to attack. Without a clear idea of where the enemy was, Lee felt he could not risk a flanking movement to the south. With the two armies at such close quarters, he knew that the Union scouts would detect his troop movements. If Meade had troops in reserve—as was very possible—the Union general could trap and annihilate Lee's flanking force.

When the fighting at Gettysburg had mushroomed into a major battle, Lee realized that retreating to a new position would be admitting he had lost the battle. Lee believed that this would be a severe blow to the Confederate cause and would encourage the victory-starved North to continue its war effort.

"No, the enemy is there and I am going to fight him there," Lee declared as he discussed his options with his advisers. As at Chancellorsville, Lee showed a willingness to take a bold risk. He based this decision on his confidence in his army.

Lee ordered George Pickett's division, reinforced from other divisions, to charge the Union center on Cemetery Ridge. He ordered a massive artillery attack to clear the way for Pickett. Stuart was to slash at the Union rear with his cavalry, and Ewell was to continue to attack Culp's Hill.

*More than 130 years after the Battle of Gettysburg,
General Robert E. Lee is still widely revered for his
courage and leadership.*

RESULT

The attack on July 3 was poorly coordinated. Ewell's men found themselves in an exposed location, and the Union troops drew them into a fight earlier than planned. Their assault failed and was over before Pickett's charge ever began. Union troops drove off Stuart's cavalry with little difficulty. As a result, Meade did not have to pull any troops out of the center to strengthen other positions.

In the heaviest artillery attack of the war, 140 Confederate cannons blazed away at the center of the Union forces. But the Confederates aimed too high and most of their cannonballs flew over the heads of the Union soldiers.

These failures meant that Pickett's 15,000 men had to charge over a half mile uphill across exposed ground into concentrated enemy fire. With incredible courage, the Confederate troops made the attempt. Union cannons and muskets shredded their ranks, yet Pickett's men continued to advance forward. The men of the Army of Northern Virginia fell in droves. The survivors finally had to give up the task as hopeless and retreat.

Approximately 20,000 soldiers from the Army of Northern Virginia—almost one-third of the Confederate fighting force—were killed or wounded during the Battle of Gettysburg. While the Union army lost 23,000 men during the three days of fighting, they could more easily replace the losses with new recruits.

The defeat at Gettysburg forced Lee to abandon his northern offensive outpost. He retreated skillfully to the South and managed to escape with most of his

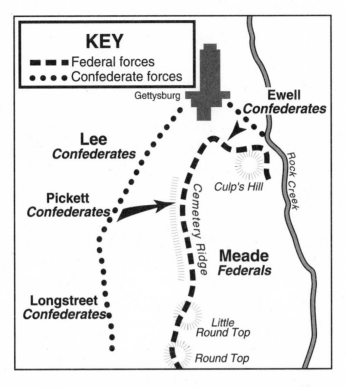

By the third day of the Battle of Gettysburg, what became known as the Union's "fishhook" defensive position was in place.

KEY
■ ■ ■ Federal forces
• • • • Confederate forces

Gettysburg

Ewell
Confederates

Lee
Confederates

Pickett
Confederates

Culp's Hill

Rock Creek

Cemetery Ridge

Meade
Federals

Longstreet
Confederates

Little
Round Top

Round Top

battered army intact. This loss, however, along with the South's defeat during the Battle of Vicksburg, Mississippi, on the same day, spelled doom for the Confederacy. Although the Civil War continued for two more years, the outcome was never in doubt after the Union's decisive victory at Gettysburg. Four months later, on November 19, 1863, the field where the Battle of Gettysburg had taken place was dedicated as a national cemetery by President Abraham Lincoln.

ANALYSIS

Lee was in a tight spot during the Battle of Gettysburg, but he had worked out of tight spots before. Longstreet's flanking suggestion may have been the best of a series of poor options. Lee might well have chosen this course even if he had been aware of the location of Union troops. But while Lee routinely took chances, he thought that taking a risk without knowing the situation was foolish.

Longstreet saw clearly that a frontal attack against the Union positions was hopeless. As he watched Pickett's troops assemble, he thought, "No 15,000 men ever arranged for battle can take that position." When the

By the end of July 4, 1863, General Robert E. Lee withdrew his forces from Gettysburg, and the Union had won its greatest victory of the Civil War.

During the Civil War, approximately 258,000 Confederate soldiers and 360,000 Union men lost their lives.

men were ready for the charge, Longstreet was asked by Pickett if his troops should advance. Bound to his orders but fearing the result, Longstreet could not speak. He could only nod his head.

Because of his confidence in his army, Lee did not foresee the result of Pickett's charge. At Gettysburg, Lee fell victim to his own pattern of success. The Confederate army had won so many impressive victories against stiff odds that both Lee and his troops began to have an unrealistic view of what they could accomplish.

General Meade also deserves credit for defending against Lee's attack. Unlike Lee's previous opponents, Meade kept his head during the course of the battle and made no major mistakes. On the eve of Pickett's charge,

Meade told his officers that he thought Lee would attack the Union center on Cemetery Ridge.

Despite the overwhelming odds against Pickett's charge, Lee believed that it failed only because of poor execution. "If it had been supported properly, it would have succeeded," he said afterward. Later, Lee also stated that he would have won the Battle of Gettysburg if Stonewall Jackson had still been alive.

Nevertheless, Lee did not try to dodge criticism for his disastrous defeat at Gettysburg. "It's all my fault," he declared shortly after the battle.

Lincoln's Gettysburg Address is perhaps the most quoted speech in U.S. history. About the battlefield Lincoln said: "We have come to dedicate a portion of that field, as a final resting place for those who here gave their lives that the nation might live."

7

THE UNITED STATES ARMY AT THE LITTLE BIGHORN
June 1876

A clash of cultures has caused several native Indian tribes and U.S. settlers to remain enemies throughout much of this century. The Indians, who occupied the region long before the first European settlers had reached North America, have sought to maintain control over their hunting grounds and homelands. White settlers, on the other hand, wish to expand their farming, gold mining, and railroad interests into the land that the Indians have been using.

The outbursts of violence between the two groups have not raged into a formal war. Instead, the fighting has consisted largely of isolated incidents—raids, counter-raids, and massacres—that flare up suddenly and end just as quickly.

The potential for serious trouble, however, is now higher than ever. A loose confederation of seven North American tribes, known collectively as the Sioux Nation, is furious at U.S. settlers for encroaching on lands guaranteed to them in an 1868 treaty—especially the sacred Black Hills, where gold was discovered in 1874. In defiance of U.S. demands, the Sioux (also called the Dakota) have refused to settle on the reservations that the U.S. government has set aside for them. Large numbers of Sioux now live in the region west of the Black Hills, near the Yellowstone and Little Bighorn rivers.

The U.S. government has sent two military units into the area to force the Sioux out of the Yellowstone region and back onto the reservations. Your scouts have discovered evidence that a large Sioux village lies in a valley just beyond the ridge. No one expects the Sioux to leave their homes peacefully.

THE OPPOSING FORCES

Based on reports from your scouts, the village may have about 12,000 residents, with as many as 4,000 warriors. One scout has caught sight of the large number of horses kept by the village. He says, flatly, "That's the biggest pony herd any man ever saw together."

The Sioux probably have as good a light cavalry force as exists in the world. They are good horseback riders, although they usually fight on foot. They fight hard with bows and arrows, clubs, knives, and rifles. Their skill in open battle is often astounding. They are also adept at hiding outdoors and preparing an ambush.

After numerous skirmishes with U.S. soldiers, thousands of Sioux agreed to relocate peacefully to reservations during the late 1860s—but many of the Indians are unwilling to give up even more of their land to white settlers.

Nevertheless, the Sioux cannot begin to match the firepower of the U.S. Army. They have few guns or rifles, and they have been able to obtain no heavy artillery.

When the Sioux go into battle, they do not assign warriors to units or divisions that perform assigned duties. They honor and respect their chiefs, such as Crazy Horse and Gall, and their spiritual leaders, such as Sitting Bull. But the concept of taking direct battle orders is foreign to the Sioux. They consider warfare to be primarily an individual enterprise. Each warrior is free to demonstrate his courage and skill in battle as he chooses. This system does not allow for intricate strategy and tactics.

YOUR FORCES

The United States actually has two army divisions in the vicinity. General George Crook has more than 1,000 soldiers encamped somewhere to the south of your present location. After fighting Apache Indians in Arizona in 1873, Crook is now well known as a skilled officer. General Alfred Terry commands an even larger force, which is now located to the north of your unit. In contrast to the Sioux, the U.S. Army is well equipped with rifles and ammunition.

Your 7th Cavalry unit, which is part of General Terry's force, consists of approximately 450 mounted soldiers. They are a mixture of seasoned Indian fighters and inexperienced recruits who have never been in a battle. Your force split off from Terry's command yesterday with instructions to locate the Indian gathering, to find out which way the Indians were going, and to stop any Sioux who tried to escape to the south.

Your men have now been riding southward for four days in the dry summer sun, looking for Sioux outposts. Because your primary purpose is scouting, your force is designed for speed rather than power. General Terry intends to rejoin you in this vicinity sometime tomorrow, on June 26, 1876. His men cannot move as quickly as your force on horseback because his command includes a large number of foot soldiers.

YOU ARE IN COMMAND.

Your scouts have located a Sioux village in a nearby valley. What is your next move?

Option 1 **Divide your command and attack.**

The Sioux simply do not have the firepower to stand up to the U.S. Army. As any veteran of Indian wars can tell you, the most frustrating thing about fighting the Sioux is finding them. They are incredibly mobile and adept at disappearing with hardly a trace.

You have found a huge encampment of Sioux, including many of their most skilled warriors. Such an opportunity may not come again for a long time. In fact, if you do not act quickly, all of the villagers could scatter away. Who knows how long you'll have to spend tracking them down or how many people might die before you accomplish your mission of clearing the entire Yellowstone region of Sioux?

This Sioux village lies along a valley near the Little Bighorn River. If you attack from one end only, most of the village could easily escape out the other end. To prevent this, you need to send part of your force across the ridge and around to the back of the encampment while the other part attacks directly in front of the village.

Dividing your small force is, of course, a risky military maneuver. But fighting Indians is nothing like the type of battles for which military academies prepare soldiers. Previous U.S. cavalry battles have shown that a sudden attack in full force from more than one direction has been effective against the Indian villages on the Great Plains. The more prongs to your attack, the better chance you have of confusing the Indians. With your troops vastly outnumbered, confusion is crucial to prevent the Sioux from launching a fierce counterattack.

Option 2 **Attack but keep your cavalry together.**

Although you want to strike immediately before the Sioux have a chance to scatter, you must consider the size of this encampment. Previous cavalry attacks against Indian villages have never faced the steep odds that you are up against. Even allowing for the fact that your frightened scouts may be exaggerating, you have to figure that within the camp are as many as 4,000 Sioux warriors. That means the Sioux warriors could outnumber your 7th Cavalry by almost nine to one.

The Indians may be poorly armed and short on ammunition, but given their sharp battle skills, the odds are tough for you to beat. The last thing you want to do is risk making those odds worse. What if part of your command were to get ambushed by part of the Sioux force or bogged down in a slow advance? That could leave the rest of the Sioux village free to swarm over the other part of your command. While you may have confidence in your men, they are not invincible.

Consider the terrain, as well. Although the countryside has few trees, deep *ravines*—narrow gorges in the earth—cut through the hills in many places. Many Sioux warriors could easily hide in these ravines and set deadly ambushes against your men.

For the safety of your soldiers, you must keep them together against such a strong enemy force. This will not allow you to trap the Sioux in the valley, and the bulk of them may escape. But, realistically, what are the chances of your small force of 450 soldiers bottling up 4,000 Sioux warriors—along with 8,000 other Sioux villagers? There is also a good chance that the Sioux will retreat straight into the path of General Terry and his troops coming down from the north.

Option 3 **Watch the Sioux but do not attack until Terry arrives.**

You cannot afford to take the Sioux lightly. Other commanders have made that error—and died because of their mistake. In December 1866, an arrogant U.S. Army officer named William Fetterman charged into an Indian force that was much larger than his own. Led by Chief Red Cloud, the enraged Sioux killed Fetterman and the more than 80 men under his command.

Your cavalry is better outfitted for scouting missions and swift skirmishes than for a major battle against the vast Indian encampment in the valley. No one would expect your force to take on the Sioux alone, nor do you have any need to do so. General Terry's force will arrive in the vicinity within a day or so. All you have to do is maintain surveillance on the Sioux village and, given its size, that should not be difficult. When Terry arrives, you can coordinate a battle plan with him. A combined attack would give you a far better chance of success. If the Sioux gathering begins to scatter, you can split your command to go after the various bands.

Option 4 **Withdraw from the area and rejoin Terry.**

Your scouts are convinced that you and your soldiers are in grave danger. This powerful concentration of Sioux near the Little Bighorn may be one of the strongest fighting forces of Indians every assembled.

While some other U.S. cavalry units have in the past been able to escape detection by Indians in the Great Plains, that generally happened with small villages that expected no trouble from whites. The chances that a huge encampment of hostile Sioux will fail to detect your presence in this open country are slim. The longer you linger near this valley, the greater the risk that the Sioux will attack you. If that happens, your men will have to flee for their lives.

Remember, the Sioux have an enormous herd of ponies feeding in the valley. These animals are alert and ready to run. Your horses, on the other hand, have been pushed hard for four days, and many of your animals are near exhaustion. If the Sioux ride out in force against you, their fresh mounts should have no trouble outrunning your tired horses.

Your scouts clearly want nothing to do with the Indian force in the valley. Veteran scout Mitch Bouyer, who knows this country as well as any white man, says bluntly, "Get your outfit out of the country as fast as your played-out horses can carry you."

After several territorial conflicts with the U.S. Army during the 1860s, the Sioux Indians of the Great Plains agreed to stay in the Black Hills region. Now that gold has been discovered there, the United States government wants the Indians to relocate again.

THE DECISION IS YOURS.
WHAT WILL YOU DO?

Option 1   **Divide your command and attack.**

Option 2   **Attack but keep your cavalry together.**

Option 3   **Watch the Sioux but do not attack until Terry arrives.**

Option 4   **Withdraw from the area and rejoin Terry.**

Cavalry leader George Armstrong Custer (1839-1876), who had gained impressive military credentials during the Civil War, hoped to add to his fame by defeating the Indians.

Lieutenant-Colonel George Custer chose *Option 1*.

George Armstrong Custer of the U.S. Cavalry was worried that if he did not attack immediately, the Sioux gathering would disband. The various Sioux tribes would sneak away into the hills and out of the reach of the U.S. Army. He dismissed his scouts' warnings about the large size of the Sioux camp. He had once told an audience at a luncheon in New York that his regiment alone could whip all the Indians on the Great Plains.

Custer, who knew he might be nominated as a presidential candidate at the Democratic National Convention later that month, actually welcomed being badly outnumbered because he thought a difficult victory would increase his popularity. If he could send news of a glorious military victory to the convention, he would greatly boost his chances of being nominated for president.

Custer's only previous action against Plains Indians had been an early morning charge against a southern Cheyenne village at the Washita River (in what is now Oklahoma) in November 1868. His experience at that earlier encounter, along with an outstanding performance as a Union officer in the Civil War, told him that the best way to defeat a strong encampment was to attack from several sides at once.

Custer divided his force of 450 men into three sections. He ordered one unit, led by Major Marcus Reno, to ride into the valley and attack the village. With a promise to support Reno, Custer led the main force along a ridge to the right of the village. A third section, under Captain Frederick Benteen, rode into the hills to the left.

Major Marcus Reno was one of Custer's most loyal men. Like many military officers, he was willing to risk his life for his commanding officer.

RESULT

As Reno charged the village, he realized the Sioux were far stronger than his relatively tiny force of 112 troopers. Furthermore, he recognized that the Sioux were moving back easily, drawing his men into an ambush. Reno ordered his men to dismount and form a short battle line. Suffering heavy casualties at the hands of an overpowering enemy force, Reno's command retreated into a woods and then up to a hilltop. There they fought desperately, trying to hold out until Custer arrived. Custer, meanwhile, rode along the ridge toward the Little Bighorn River. Before he got there, numerous Sioux warriors swarmed over the army's left side and rear.

To the Sioux, this battle was far more than a test of individual skill and courage. They were fighting to defend the thousands of unarmed women and children in their village. Heeding the advice of leaders such as Crazy Horse and Gall to forego reckless charges, they concentrated on sealing off Custer's troops from escape.

The Sioux pinned down Custer's men on a low ridge that offered the cavalrymen no protection. Within a half hour, the Indians overwhelmed Custer's force of about

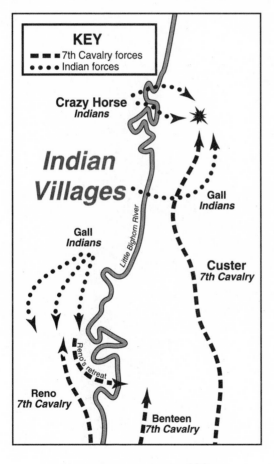

Underestimating the strength of his Indian enemies, Custer divided his command three ways (under Reno, Benteen, and himself), and left his entire force severely weakened.

At the Little Bighorn, the Sioux under Crazy Horse wiped out Custer and every man with him.

200 men, killing every one of them. This historic battle is now often called "Custer's Last Stand."

Reno's men, meanwhile, were well on their way to a similar fate until Captain Benteen disregarded his orders and returned in time to join the beleaguered unit. Even with the addition of Benteen's 120 soldiers, the remaining members of the 7th Cavalry were hopelessly trapped. But instead of risking losses by storming the enemy, the Sioux decided to let thirst do the job for them. Reno's men suffered terribly from lack of water because the Sioux fired at them whenever they moved toward the Little Bighorn River. Fortunately for them, the Sioux broke camp and left the battle site before Reno's men died of thirst.

The Indians' stunning victory at Little Bighorn did not alter their bleak prospects for the future. With a superior supply of weapons and an overwhelmingly larger population, the United States was able to end the resistance of the Plains Indians within a few years and force thousands of them to move to small reservations.

ANALYSIS

George Custer showed little interest in or respect for his opponents during the Battle of the Little Bighorn. Among his troops, Custer had a reputation for reckless behavior—riding first and scouting later. He had always gotten away with this tactic, a fact that many soldiers attributed to "Custer luck." At the Little Bighorn, his luck ran out, and he and his men paid the price for his rash behavior.

Given the overwhelming odds against him and his unfamiliarity with an area that was ripe with ambush possibilities, Custer's decision to divide his forces was inexcusable. He compounded this blunder by sending Benteen's detachment off into the hills, away from the likely fighting. If Benteen had followed his orders to the letter, he would have been too far off to save the rest of Reno's men.

In the midst of the fight, one of Reno's men, Captain Myles Moylan, remarked, "In my opinion, Custer has made the biggest mistake of his life not taking the whole regiment at once into the first attack." Many historians agree, often calling the Battle of the Little Bighorn one of the worst military actions in U.S. history.

The combined units of Reno and Benteen survived only because the Sioux, having satisfied their desire for revenge on Custer, chose not to take the time to finish off the rest of the U.S. troops. In a battle against the entire Sioux encampment, Custer had virtually no chance of success. Given the exhausted state of his horses, his cavalry would have been extremely lucky to escape.

Political ambition apparently drove Custer to make his fatal errors. One possible explanation for sending Benteen away was to make sure Custer's force could take credit for the expected victory, with help only from Reno. While that is merely speculation, little doubt remains that Custer's unwillingness to share the glory prompted his tragic decision to go beyond his scouting orders and attack instead of waiting for Terry's force to arrive.

After their victory at the Little Bighorn, Sitting Bull (1831?-1890) led thousands of Sioux Indians into Canada to avoid further attacks from the U.S. Army.

8

THE BOER ARMY IN NATAL
December 1899

E ver since the Dutch settlers (or *Boers*) from the Transvaal region of South Africa formed their own republic, they have sparred with the British, who claim rights to the area. Throughout the 1800s, the British have increased their territorial acquisitions in Africa. The Boers (which means "farmers") had moved into the Transvaal to establish their independence from Britain, and they naturally resented the British newcomers.

From 1877 to 1881, the Boers fought Britain's attempt to annex the Transvaal into the British Empire. Eventually the British backed off and left your people in peace. But the discovery of gold in the Transvaal in 1886 has brought an influx of British prospectors.

The resulting struggle between those who want to increase the British presence in the Transvaal and neighboring areas and those who want to maintain Boer independence has escalated into war. The Boers had seen the storm coming and were prepared when war broke out this autumn. A strong force of well-armed Boers pushed south into the British-governed province of Natal. There, they trapped the entire British Natal Field Force

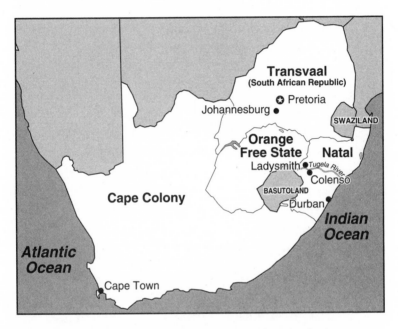

Since gaining control of the Cape Colony in the late 1700s and early 1800s, the British have tried to increase their possessions in South Africa. Suspecting that Britain intended to claim the Transvaal region, the Dutch descendants living in the Transvaal and Orange Free State joined forces in 1896 and began fighting the British three years later. A new battle is about to take place near the town of Colenso.

under General George White in the town of Ladysmith. This British force has made several attempts to break out, but has had no success. One of these attempts ended with the humiliating capture of nearly 1,000 British soldiers.

Realizing that White's command is short on food and supplies and may have to surrender soon, the British government has landed a large army in South Africa with orders to free Ladysmith. That army is now approaching from the south. Your Boer army has the task of stopping the British reinforcements from breaking the Boer siege of Ladysmith.

THE OPPOSING FORCES

The British army has perhaps been the world's best military force for most of the nineteenth century. This superior might has allowed Great Britain to expand its empire and increase its power around the globe. Success has made the army very confident. British infantrymen uphold a tradition of being among the most disciplined and courageous soldiers in the world.

These troops have a weakness, however, and that is a continued reliance on old military practices. They continue to march into an attack in tightly bunched columns and depend on soldiers armed with *bayonets*, or blades attached to rifle muzzles.

These tactics, which once worked so well for the British, are now outdated. Accurate, long-range rifles (which soldiers can reload quickly) have changed the rules of warfare. A closely packed army offers an easy target for murderous fire. Soldiers assaulting strongly held positions in mass ranks rarely get close enough to make use of their bayonets.

The British have 12,000 men at Ladysmith. They are caught in a poor position, as shown by their repeated failures to break your siege of the city. The British army marching in relief of Ladysmith is probably the finest force Great Britain has sent into action since the Crimean War of the 1850s.

More than 20,000 well-armed men are approaching your positions. These soldiers follow the command of General Redvers Buller. Popular with his men, Buller built a solid reputation as a fighter in the Kafir Zulu wars in South Africa during the late 1870s. His army is approaching Ladysmith from the southeast and preparing to assault your positions along the Tugela River near the small town of Colenso, about 12 miles from Ladysmith.

YOUR FORCES

A division of roughly 10,000 Boer soldiers has entrapped White's 12,000 soldiers at Ladysmith. This Boer army commands dominating positions from the hills that encircle the town.

You currently have 6,000 soldiers under your command—about one-tenth the total number of men in the Boer army. Although the British don't have much respect for the Boer soldiers, the Boers tend to be rugged fighters and excellent marksmen with a strong sense of national unity. Unlike the British troops, they do not take orders easily, and they do not like to stand up in the open during combat. "Lie low and don't waste ammunition" is their military creed. They have serviceable weapons and are able to move quickly from one spot to another.

You have positioned your men in well-concealed trenches along seven miles of hills north of the Tugela River. Your strongest positions are centered on the railroad bridges that span the river near the town of Colenso. There is a shallow spot—or *ford*—in the Tugela several miles to the west. If the British were to cross there, they might be able to squeeze you between two attacking forces.

On the east, a towering hill called Hlangwane (pronounced *shlang-wahn-ee*) presents a puzzling dilemma. The hill rises more than 3,600 feet above the surrounding

The British considered Boer soldiers (above) to be undisciplined ruffians because most of them lacked official uniforms and formal military training.

land and provides a commanding view of the terrain. If the British were to seize this hill, they could see into some of your carefully concealed defensive outposts.

Unfortunately, the river runs between Hlangwane and the rest of your defensive positions on the other side of the river. Any troops you stationed on Hlangwane would be dangerously exposed, and you would be unable to provide reinforcements quickly. Worse yet, a strong enemy advance could surround the hill and cut off any possible escape for your soldiers.

YOU ARE IN COMMAND.

How will you stop Buller's force from arriving at Ladysmith?

Option 1 Commit a large number of troops to defend Hlangwane.

A basic rule of battlefield management is to control the high ground. Hlangwane so dominates the landscape that it holds the key to your success. If you lose it, you may have great difficulty holding your positions.

You are already only 12 miles from Ladysmith, where 12,000 British soldiers hope to assist Buller's attempt to break through the Boer siege. If you lose the hill and have to retreat, you allow the two British forces to grow closer, increasing the chance that they can coordinate their efforts against you and the rest of the Boer army.

The British surely recognize the value of Hlangwane and are likely to commit a strong force to capturing it.

You must be certain your forces on the hill are strong enough to defend it.

Option 2 **Station a small force on Hlangwane and concentrate on keeping your center strong.**

While Hlangwane is important, you have other concerns that are equally pressing. If you commit too many soldiers to the hill, your strength elsewhere will be diminished.

The most likely place for the British to attack is straight ahead, particularly if you can lure them into such a move by remaining hidden. The British are too confident of their military superiority over what they consider to be a ragged bunch of farmers. That means they will probably take the shortest and most direct route to their objective—Ladysmith.

Another factor you must keep in mind is the difficulty of escaping from Hlangwane. While you need to defend the hill, you must think twice about committing too large a portion of your force to a place where the British can easily surround your troops and prevent them from escaping.

Your best move, then, is to keep the bulk of your forces hidden in a strong defensive position centered on Colenso and send a smaller force to hold Hlangwane as long as possible. The steepness of the climb should hinder the British advance up the hill and allow a small Boer force to defend it well.

Option 3 **Shift your forces to the west.**

The British are not amateurs at warfare. They must realize that you hold a strong position in the hills north of the Tugela River. Your forces are so well hidden that the British cannot even see them. The British would surely look for an alternative to massing a costly attack against this sector.

Similarly, the British must realize the importance of Hlangwane to your army. They would expect you to hold the hill tenaciously and, therefore, should be looking for a less costly route of advance. Such a route exists several miles to the west, where the Tugela River is much shallower. If the British get there while you sit still, they will be able to seize the hills to the west and come in behind your well-laid defenses. Most likely, you would then have to abandon your positions. Therefore, you would be wise to shift the majority of your men to meet the potential threat. The British would decline to make that move only if they feared lengthening their supply lines to the west or leaving the rest of Natal exposed to Boer attacks.

Option 4 **Abandon your siege and begin guerrilla warfare.**

Your position is not as strong as it first appeared. Hlangwane poses a big problem to you. Because the hill is on the wrong side of the river, Buller and the British could throw all their strength at it and overwhelm it before attacking your center. The soldiers you had stationed on Hlangwane are well aware of this. They have already abandoned the hill and refuse to go back up it.

You will not have an easy time defending the hills if Buller shifts to the west. Worst of all, regardless of where he attacks, the British troops that you have bottled up in Ladysmith will attempt to help him. They will surely make some attempt to charge from the rear.

The entire Boer army in South Africa numbers only 60,000. Even at full strength, your army could not defeat a British army, which could raise 400,000 soldiers in an emergency. When facing an enemy with vastly superior resources, you are better off conducting a hit-and-run *guerrilla* campaign. You must keep striking and keep moving, never giving battle. That way, the British will exhaust thousands of troops in trying to put an end to your rebellion. Eventually, they may tire of the whole business and leave your republic alone.

THE DECISION IS YOURS.
WHAT WILL YOU DO?

Option 1	**Commit a large number of troops to defend Hlangwane.**
Option 2	**Station a small force on Hlangwane and concentrate on keeping your center strong.**
Option 3	**Shift your forces to the west.**
Option 4	**Abandon your siege and begin guerrilla warfare.**

General Louis Botha chose *Option 2*.

Although Louis Botha had strong political skills, he had limited military experience prior to taking command of the Boer army. At first, he argued for abandoning the positions and taking his entire army on a march through the province of Natal. He thought he could strike terror into the British by invading all the way to the coastal city of Durban. But advisers persuaded him to forget this notion.

In preparing to repel the British attack, Botha said, "My first idea was that the position I believed about to be assaulted should be strengthened in such a manner as to be unknown to the enemy." He thought the overconfident British "would march straight down the railroad tracks," into the center of the Boer defense. Botha had his army prepare gun pits and trenches and hidden barbed wire so they could have thousands of riflemen blazing away at the British troops from protected positions. These soldiers stayed hidden and refused to respond when the British fired shots into the hills.

Botha also decided that he must defend Hlangwane and pleaded with his soldiers to return to their post. When they refused to listen, he appealed to Paul Kruger, the president of the Boers. Kruger supported Botha's decision and ordered the Boer soldiers to defend the hill. Botha, however, committed only 600 of his men to protect the hill. The Boer soldiers drew lots to see who would have to fight on Hlangwane.

After the Boer War ended, Louis Botha (1862-1919) became an important political leader in South Africa, serving as the nation's prime minister from 1910 until his death.

Behind the lines of the British army at the Battle of Colenso in December 1899

RESULT

British general Buller surveyed the situation and decided that "a direct assault upon the enemy position at Colenso and north of it would be too costly." Therefore, he prepared his army to march to the shallow crossing to the west. He sent word to General White at Ladysmith to coordinate his attack with Buller's intended attack on December 17, 1899.

Buller, however, suddenly changed his mind and proceeded to do exactly what Botha had predicted. He canceled the marching orders and decided to make a direct assault against Boer positions. He attacked on December 15—two days earlier than he had planned—without informing the Ladysmith contingent. Buller paid little attention to Hlangwane and sent a small force of mounted troops to take the position. Botha's force reappeared on the hill just hours before this British unit began to charge.

The British attack collapsed quickly into a series of embarrassing blunders. The British soldiers lost track of where they were. In their eagerness to shell the Boers, they rushed forward, almost to the Boer battle fortifications. The hidden Boer sharpshooters began picking off the gunners, who were preparing to fire their cannons. Buller spent so much time and effort trying to retrieve the cannons that he neglected to proceed with the rest of the attack.

The left wing of the British attack could not find the shallow ford in the river. British soldiers stumbled into a bend of the Tugela River where the hidden Boers poured their rifle fire at them from three sides. Some British struggled across the deep river only to run into barbed wire hidden beneath the surface of the water.

The British soldiers at Colenso nearly captured Hlangwane. But when Colonel Lord Dundonald drew near the crest and called for reinforcements to carry him over the top, he received no reply from Buller. Seeing the bloody fate of his men in the river, Buller lost his nerve and ordered a retreat. Dundonald lost more men in retreating from Hlangwane than he had lost in nearly reaching the top.

The British suffered an unexpected defeat at Colenso. Their losses were 143 men dead, more than 750 wounded, and nearly 250 captured. The well-sheltered Boers suffered only 8 deaths and 30 wounded. The defeat so shattered Buller that he signaled to General White at Ladysmith, "I suggest your firing away as much ammunition as you can, and making the best terms that you can."

Coming on the heels of two other British defeats at the hands of the Boers in the same week, the defeat at Colenso shocked the British. They referred to this period as the "Black Week." Eager to restore pride to the British Empire, thousands of young men from Great Britain—as well as the British territories of Australia, New Zealand, and Canada—enlisted in the British army. This huge force quickly overpowered the remaining Boer field army and forced the Boers to resort to guerrilla warfare, breaking off into smaller units. Buller was replaced because of his defeat during the battle.

ANALYSIS

Had Buller continued moving to the west, Botha would probably have had to abandon his positions at Colenso. British military analysts almost unanimously agree that if Buller had captured Hlangwane, the Boers would have been hard pressed to halt the British advance during the Battle of Colenso. Buller's claim that the possession of Hlangwane "did not in any way assist the crossing" has astounded military experts.

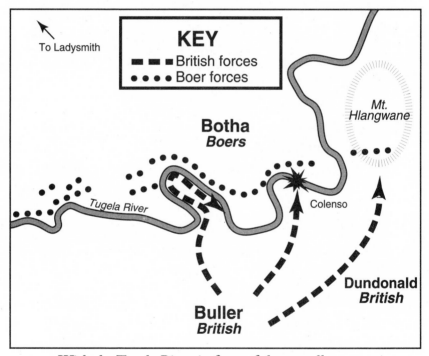

With the Tugela River in front of them, well-fortified Boer sharpshooters rained murderous fire upon the advancing British.

Despite their uniforms and formal military training, the British soldiers in South Africa had great difficulty in subduing the Boer irregulars.

Historians are no more sympathetic to Buller's explanation that he stopped shifting his forces to the west for fear of being cut off from the rest of Natal. Buller, though, rejected both options and his change of mind played perfectly into Botha's hands. He compounded his blunder by failing to notify General White at Ladysmith. Unaware of Buller's plans, White and his garrison at Ladysmith could not aid the attack. Botha was able to defend Hlangwane with only a 600-man commando unit while concentrating deadly fire on the British frontal assault.

The result at Colenso was what British general Neville Littleton termed "one of the most unfortunate battles in which a British army has ever been engaged." Littleton went on to say that "in none has there been a more deplorable tactical display."

The event would have been even more disastrous had White accepted Buller's instructions to surrender his entire force of 12,000 men. Fortunately for the British, White declined.

While Botha's strategy led to a smashing victory at Colenso, many analysts believe the Boers would have been better off abandoning Ladysmith and reverting to guerrilla warfare. Indeed, the Colenso defeat only stiffened British determination to defeat the Boers. Military historians, however, do not consider the defeat a "disaster" for the British. Rather, they call it a "serious reverse"—meaning that the British lost the battle but not any territory.

When the Boers finally did resort to guerrilla warfare, they confounded more than 400,000 British soldiers in an increasingly unpopular war. The Boers' hit-and-run tactics so exasperated the British army that the British began burning Boer farms and imprisoning women and children. These measures further eroded support from the British populace.

In 1902, the British government approved a peace agreement that eventually allowed the entire area of South Africa to become a Boer republic, which is what the Boers were fighting for in the first place.

SOURCE NOTES

Quoted passages are noted by page and order of citation:

p. 10: Forrest McDonald. *The Presidency of Thomas Jefferson.* (Lawrence: University of Kansas, 1976.)

p. 15: Samuel Carter. *Blaze of Glory: The Fight for New Orleans, 1814-1815.* (New York: St. Martin's Press, 1971.)

p. 22: Robin Reilly. *The British at the Gates: The New Orleans Campaign in the War of 1812.* (Norwalk, CT: Easton Press, 1990.)

p. 35: Bernard Law Montgomery. *A History of Warfare.* (Cleveland: World Publishing, 1968.)

pp. 43-44: J.F.C. Fuller. *The Decisive Battles of the Western World, 1792-1944.* (London: Paladin, 1970.)

pp. 59 (1st), 60 (2nd): David Nevin. *The Mexican War.* (Alexandria: Time-Life, 1978.)

pp. 59 (2nd), 60: Robert Leckie. *The Wars of America.* (New York: Harper & Row, 1980.)

p. 78 (both): Philip Warner. *The Crimean War: A Reappraisal.* (New York: Taplinger, 1973.)

pp. 90, 93: Ernest B. Furgurson. *Chancellorsville 1863: The Souls of the Brave.* (New York: Knopf, 1992.)

pp. 95, 98: William Goolrich. *Rebels Resurgent: Fredericksburg to Chancellorsville.* (Alexandria: Time-Life, 1985.)

pp. 96, 116 (both): Bruce Catton. *Gettysburg: The Final Fury.* (New York: Doubleday, 1974.)

pp. 118, 131: Mari Sandoz. *The Battle of the Little Bighorn.* (Philadelphia: Lippincott, 1966.)

pp. 142 (1st), 146, 147, 149: Kenneth Griffith. *Thank God We Kept the Flag Flying: The Siege and Relief of Ladysmith, 1899-1900.* (New York: Viking Press, 1971.)

pp. 142 (2nd), 145: Byron Farwell. *The Great Anglo-Boer War.* (New York: Harper & Row, 1976.)

BIBLIOGRAPHY

Barbary, James. *The Crimean War.* New York: Hawthorn, 1970.

Barnett, Correlli. *Britain and Her Army, 1509-1970.* New York: Morrow, 1970.

Carter, Samuel. *Blaze of Glory: The Fight for New Orleans, 1814-1815.* New York: St. Martin's Press, 1971.

Catton, Bruce. *Gettysburg: The Final Fury.* New York: Doubleday, 1974.

Cross, Robin, ed. *Warfare: A Chronological History.* London: Wellfleet, 1991.

Dupuy, Trevor N., and R. Ernest Dupuy. *The Harper Encyclopedia of Military History.* New York: Harper Collins, 1993.

Farwell, Byron. *The Great Anglo-Boer War.* New York: Harper & Row, 1976.

Fuller, J. F. C. *The Decisive Battles of the Western World, 1792-1944.* London: Paladin, 1970.

Furgurson, Ernest B. *Chancellorsville 1863: The Souls of the Brave.* New York: Knopf, 1992.

Goolrich, William. *Rebels Resurgent: Fredericksburg to Chancellorsville.* Alexandria: Time-Life, 1985.

Griffith, Kenneth. *Thank God We Kept the Flag Flying: The Siege and Relief of Ladysmith, 1899-1900.* New York: Viking Press, 1971.

Howarth, David. *Waterloo: Day of Battle*. New York: Atheneum, 1968.

Johnson, Swafford. *History of the U.S. Cavalry.* Greenwich: Crescent, 1985.

Leckie, Robert. *The Wars of America*. New York: Harper & Row, 1980.

Lee, Emanuel. *To The Bitter End: A Photographic History of the Boer War, 1899-1902*. New York: Viking Press, 1985.

McDonald, Forrest. *The Presidency of Thomas Jefferson*. Lawrence: University of Kansas, 1976.

McPherson, James. *Battle Cry of Freedom: The Civil War Era*. New York: Oxford University Press, 1988.

Montgomery, Bernard Law. *A History of Warfare*. Cleveland: World Publishing, 1968.

Nevin, David. *The Mexican War.* Alexandria: Time-Life, 1978.

Pakenham, Thomas. *The Boer War*. New York: Random House, 1979.

Reilly, Robin. *The British at the Gates: The New Orleans Campaign in the War of 1812*. Norwalk, CT: Easton Press, 1990.

Sandoz, Mari. *The Battle of the Little Bighorn*. Philadelphia: Lippincott, 1966.

Shrader, Charles Reginald. *Reference Guide to United States Military History*. New York: Facts on File, 1991.

Warner, Philip. *The Crimean War: A Reappraisal*. New York: Taplinger, 1973.

INDEX

allies (Crimean War), 64, 66, 68, 70, 71, 73, 74, 75, 76, 78

Alma River, Battle of, 64, 65, 66, 67, 68, 69, 73, 76, 78

Antietam, Battle of, 80-81

Apaches, 120

Arizona, 62, 120

army, British: in Battle of New Orleans, 10-11, 12, 13-14, 15, 16, 19, 21-23, 24-25, 26; in Battle of Waterloo, 28-29, 30, 32, 34, 35, 36-37, 40-41, 43; in Boer War, 134, 135-136, 138, 139, 140, 141, 145-146, 148-149; in Crimean War, 64, 66, 67, 69, 73-75, 136

army, French, 9, 12, 13, 20, 39; at Battle of Waterloo, 30, 32, 34, 35-37, 40-41, 43, 44; under Bonaparte, 27-28, 30; in Crimean War, 64, 65, 66, 67, 69-70, 73-75

army, Russian, 64, 65, 67-68, 69-70, 73, 74, 75, 78

Army, U.S.: in Battle of Little Big Horn, 118, 120-122, 123-124, 127-132; in Battle of New Orleans, 10, 11, 12-13, 14, 15, 16, 17, 19, 21-22, 23, 24-25, 26, 45; in

Mexican War, 45, 47, 48, 49, 50-52, 54-57, 59, 60, 61-62. *See also* Union army

Army of Northern Virginia, 81, 87, 99, 100, 103, 107, 112

Army of the North, 30

artillery, use of: in Battle of New Orleans, 16, 17, 21, 22; in Civil War, 91, 109, 110, 112; in Crimean War, 69, 71, 78; at Little Big Horn, 119; in Mexican War, 50, 52. *See also* cannons, use of

Balaclava, 73, 74

bayonets, 135

Belgium, 29, 32

Benteen, Captain Frederick, 127, 130, 131, 132

Beyers, Fort, 19

Black Hills, 118, 125

Black Sea, 63, 64, 66, 71

Black Week, 146

Blücher, Marshall Gebhard von: background of, 38, 39; decisions of, in Battle of Waterloo, 39, 43; as military leader, 39, 41, 43, 44; options of, in Battle of Waterloo, 34-37

Boers: army of, 134, 135,

Guadalupe Hidalgo, Treaty of,
62
guerrilla warfare, 141, 146, 149
gunboats, 10. *See also* warships

Hlangwane hill, 137-139, 140,
142, 145, 146, 147
Hooker, Joseph, 83-85, 87, 88,
89, 90-91, 93, 101-102; at
Battle of Chancellorsville,
94-95, 97-98, 99, 106

Indians, American: conflict of,
with whites, 45, 117-118,
119, 123, 125, 127; forces of,
at Little Big Horn, 118-120,
121. *See also* Sioux Nation
Inkerman, 74

Jackson, Andrew, 12, 13, 14,
15-16, 17-19, 21, 22, 24-26
Jackson, Thomas "Stonewall,"
86, 90, 93, 94-95, 96, 97,
103, 108, 116; death of, 104
Jefferson, Thomas, 10

Kafir Zulu wars, 136
Kamiesch, 73, 74
Keane, John, 22-23
Kruger, Paul, 142

Ladysmith, 135, 136, 138, 139,
145, 146, 148; military
options in defending, 138-
141; opposing forces at, 135-
138; siege of, 135, 136, 138,
141
Lafitte, Jean, 12, 13
Lee, Major-General Robert E.,
60; background of, 92, 93;
decisions of, at
Chancellorsville, 93-98;
decisions of, at Gettysburg,
110, 112-113; as military
leader, 93, 98, 111, 114;
options of, at
Chancellorsville, 87-91;
options of, at Gettysburg,
105-109, 114
Ligny, Battle of, 29, 32, 38, 40,
43
Lincoln, Abraham, 79-80, 83,
84, 101-102, 113, 116
Little Big Horn, Battle of the:
causes of, 118; military
options at, 121-125;
opposing forces at, 118-121;
outcome of, 127-132
Little Bighorn River, 118, 121,
124, 128, 130
Littleton, Neville, 149
Longstreet, Lieutenant-
General James, 85, 89, 90,
91, 105, 107, 114-115
Louisiana Territory, 10
Lyons, Sir Edmund, 69

Madison, James, 10
Meade, George, 102, 105-106,
107, 108, 110, 112, 115-116
Menschikov, Alexander, 64
Mexican War, 47, 51, 59;

George Custer's overwhelming defeat at the Little Bighorn helped to make him one of the most memorable—and controversial—figures in American history.

ABOUT THE AUTHOR

NATHAN AASENG is a widely published writer of both fiction and non-fiction books for young adults. He has covered a diverse range of subjects, including history, biography, social issues, sports, health, business, and science. Among Aaseng's books are *Great Justices of the Supreme Court, America's Third-Party Presidential Candidates, You Are the Supreme Court Justice, You Are the President, You Are the President II: 1800-1899, You Are the General,* and the forthcoming title, *Genetics: Unlocking the Secrets of Life.* He lives in Eau Claire, Wisconsin, with his wife and children.

Photo Credits